CCNP BSCI
Portable Command Guide

Scott Empson

Cisco Press

800 East 96th Street
Indianapolis, IN 46240 USA

CCNP BSCI Portable Command Guide

Scott Empson

Copyright© 2007 Cisco Systems, Inc.

The Cisco Press logo is a trademark of Cisco Systems, Inc.

Published by:
Cisco Press
800 East 96th Street
Indianapolis, IN 46240 USA

Printed in the United States of America 1 2 3 4 5 6 7 8 9 0

First Printing   May 2007

ISBN-10: 1-58720-189-5

ISBN-13: 978-1-58720-189-9

Library of Congress Cataloging-in-Publication Data

Empson, Scott.

  CCNP BSCI portable command guide / Scott Empson. -- 1st ed.

     p. cm.

  ISBN 978-1-58720-189-9 (pbk.)

  1. Computer networks--Problems, exercises, etc. 2. Internetworking (Telecommunication)--Examinations--Study guides. 3. Telecommunications engineers--Certification--Examinations--Study guides. 4. Routers (Computer networks)--Examinations--Study guides. I. Title.

  TK5105.8.C57E56 2007

  004.6--dc22

                              2007014235

Warning and Disclaimer

This book is designed to provide information about the Certified Cisco Networking Professional (CCNP) Building Scalable Cisco Internetworks (BSCI) exam and the commands needed at this level of network administration. Every effort has been made to make this book as complete and as accurate as possible, but no warranty or fitness is implied.

The information is provided on an "as is" basis. The authors, Cisco Press, and Cisco Systems, Inc. shall have neither liability nor responsibility to any person or entity with respect to any loss or damages arising from the information contained in this book or from the use of the discs or programs that may accompany it.

The opinions expressed in this book belong to the author and are not necessarily those of Cisco Systems, Inc.

Feedback Information

At Cisco Press, our goal is to create in-depth technical books of the highest quality and value. Each book is crafted with care and precision, undergoing rigorous development that involves the unique expertise of members from the professional technical community.

Readers' feedback is a natural continuation of this process. If you have any comments regarding how we could improve the quality of this book, or otherwise alter it to better suit your needs, you can contact us through e-mail at feedback@ciscopress.com. Please make sure to include the book title and ISBN in your message.

We greatly appreciate your assistance.

Corporate and Government Sales

Cisco Press offers excellent discounts on this book when ordered in quantity for bulk purchases or special sales.

For more information please contact:
U.S. Corporate and Government Sales
1-800-382-3419 corpsales@pearsontechgroup.com

For sales outside the U.S. please contact:
International Sales
international@pearsoned.com

Trademark Acknowledgments

All terms mentioned in this book that are known to be trademarks or service marks have been appropriately capitalized. Cisco Press or Cisco Systems, Inc. cannot attest to the accuracy of this information. Use of a term in this book should not be regarded as affecting the validity of any trademark or service mark.

Associate Publisher	David Dusthimer
Executive Editor	Mary Beth Ray
Cisco Representative	Anthony Wolfenden
Cisco Press Program Manager	Jeff Brady
Managing Editor	Patrick Kanouse
Senior Development Editor	Christopher Cleveland
Copy Editor	Keith Cline
Technical Editors	Tami Day-Orsatti, David Kotfila
Team Coordinator	Vanessa Evans
Designer	Louisa Adair
Composition	Mark Shirar
Proofreader	Karen A. Gill

CISCO.

Americas Headquarters	Asia Pacific Headquarters	Europe Headquarters
Cisco Systems, Inc.	Cisco Systems, Inc.	Cisco Systems International BV
170 West Tasman Drive	168 Robinson Road	Haarlerbergpark
San Jose, CA 95134-1706	#28-01 Capital Tower	Haarlerbergweg 13-19
USA	Singapore 068912	1101 CH Amsterdam
www.cisco.com	www.cisco.com	The Netherlands
Tel: 408 526-4000	Tel: +65 6317 7777	www-europe.cisco.com
800 553-NETS (6387)	Fax: +65 6317 7799	Tel: +31 0 800 020 0791
Fax: 408 527-0883		Fax: +31 0 20 357 1100

Cisco has more than 200 offices worldwide. Addresses, phone numbers, and fax numbers are listed on the Cisco Website at **www.cisco.com/go/offices.**

©2007 Cisco Systems, Inc. All rights reserved. CCVP, the Cisco logo, and the Cisco Square Bridge logo are trademarks of Cisco Systems, Inc.; Changing the Way We Work, Live, Play, and Learn is a service mark of Cisco Systems, Inc.; and Access Registrar, Aironet, BPX, Catalyst, CCDA, CCDP, CCIE, CCIP, CCNA, CCNP, CCSP, Cisco, the Cisco Certified Internetwork Expert logo, Cisco IOS, Cisco Press, Cisco Systems, Cisco Systems Capital, the Cisco Systems logo, Cisco Unity, Enterprise/Solver, EtherChannel, EtherFast, EtherSwitch, Fast Step, Follow Me Browsing, FormShare, GigaDrive, GigaStack, HomeLink, Internet Quotient, IOS, IP/TV, iQ Expertise, the iQ logo, iQ Net Readiness Scorecard, iQuick Study, LightStream, Linksys, MeetingPlace, MGX, Networking Academy, Network Registrar, Packet, PIX, ProConnect, RateMUX, ScriptShare, SlideCast, SMARTnet, StackWise, The Fastest Way to Increase Your Internet Quotient, and TransPath are registered trademarks of Cisco Systems, Inc. and/or its affiliates in the United States and certain other countries.

All other trademarks mentioned in this document or Website are the property of their respective owners. The use of the word partner does not imply a partnership relationship between Cisco and any other company. (0609R)

About the Author

Scott Empson is currently the assistant program chair of the bachelor of applied information systems technology degree program at the Northern Alberta Institute of Technology in Edmonton, Alberta, Canada, where he teaches Cisco routing, switching, and network design courses in a variety of different programs—certificate, diploma, and applied degree—at the post-secondary level. Scott is also the program coordinator of the Cisco Networking Academy Program at NAIT, a Regional Academy covering Central and Northern Alberta. He has earned three undergraduate degrees: a bachelor of arts, with a major in English; a bachelor of education, again with a major in English/language arts; and a bachelor of applied information systems technology, with a major in network management. He currently holds several industry certifications, including CCNP, CCDA, CCAI, and Network+. Prior to instructing at NAIT, he was a junior/senior high school English/language arts/computer science teacher at different schools throughout Northern Alberta. Scott lives in Edmonton, Alberta, with his wife Trina and two children, Zachariah and Shaelyn, where he enjoys reading, performing music on the weekend with his classic rock band "Miss Understood," and studying the martial art of TaeKwon-Do.

About the Technical Reviewers

Tami Day-Orsatti (CCSI, CCDP, CCNP, CISSP, MCT, MCSE 2000/2003: Security) is an IT networking and security instructor for T^2 IT Training. She is responsible for the delivery of authorized Cisco, (ISC)^2, and Microsoft classes. She has more than 23 years in the IT industry working with many different types of organizations (private business, city and federal government, and the Department of Defense), providing project management and senior-level network and security technical skills in the design and implementation of complex computing environments.

David Kotfila (CCNP, CCAI) is the director of the Cisco Academy at Rensselaer Polytechnic Institute (RPI), Troy, New York. Under his direction, more than 125 students have received their CCNP, and 6 students have obtained their CCIE. David is a consultant for Cisco, working as a member of the CCNP assessment group. His team at RPI is authoring the four new CCNP lab books for the Academy Program. David has served on the National Advisory Council for the Academy Program for four years. Previously he was the senior training manager at PSINet, a Tier 1 global ISP. When David is not staring at his beautiful wife, Kate, or talking with his two wonderful children, Chris and Charis, he likes to kayak and lift weights.

Dedications

Once again, this book is dedicated to Trina, Zach, and Shae.

Acknowledgments

Anyone who has ever had anything to do with the publishing industry knows that it takes many, many people to create a book. It might be my name on the cover, but there is no way that I can take credit for all that occurred to get this book from idea to publication. Therefore, I must thank:

The team at Cisco Press—Once again, you amaze me with your professionalism and the ability to make me look good. Mary Beth, Chris, Patrick—thank you for your continued support and belief in my little engineering journal.

To my technical reviewers, Tami and David—thanks for keeping me on track and making sure that what I wrote was correct and relevant.

To Rick Graziani—thank you for showing me how to present this material to my students in a fun and entertaining way, and in an educational manner.

Finally, big thanks go out to Hans Roth. There are not enough superlatives in the dictionary to describe Hans and his dedication to not only education, but also to the world of networking in general. While I was working on this series of books, Hans decided that he needed to leave the "ivory tower of education" and get his hands dirty again in industry. So what better way to get back into the swing of things than to go to Africa and design and help install a new converged infrastructure for an entire country? He also had enough time to listen to my ideas, make suggestions, and build most of the diagrams that are in this book. His input has always been invaluable, and for that, I thank him.

Contents at a Glance

Contents

Icons Used in This Book

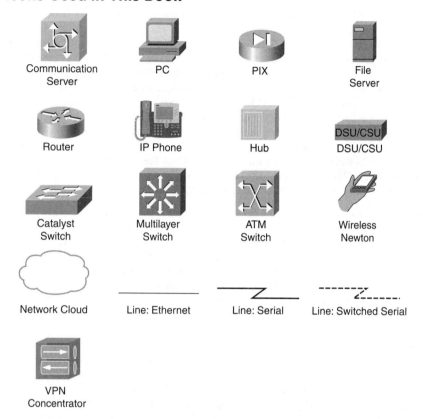

Communication Server

PC

PIX

File Server

Router

IP Phone

Hub

DSU/CSU

Catalyst Switch

Multilayer Switch

ATM Switch

Wireless Newton

Network Cloud

Line: Ethernet

Line: Serial

Line: Switched Serial

VPN Concentrator

Command Syntax Conventions

The conventions used to present command syntax in this book are the same conventions used in the IOS Command Reference. The Command Reference describes these conventions as follows:

- **Boldface** indicates commands and keywords that are entered literally as shown. In actual configuration examples and output (not general command syntax), boldface indicates commands that are manually input by the user (such as a **show** command).
- *Italics* indicate arguments for which you supply actual values.
- Vertical bars (|) separate alternative, mutually exclusive elements.
- Square brackets [ ] indicate optional elements.
- Braces { } indicate a required choice.
- Braces within brackets [{ }] indicate a required choice within an optional element.

Introduction

Welcome to third major iteration of the CCNP certification! In the spring of 2006, Cisco Press came to me and told me, albeit quietly, that there was going to be a major revision of the CCNP certification exams. They then asked whether I would be interested in working on a command guide in the same fashion as my previous books for Cisco Press: the Cisco Networking Academy Program *CCNA Command Quick Reference*, and the *CCNA Portable Command Guide*. The original idea was to create a single-volume command summary for all four of the new CCNP exams. However, early on in my research, I quickly discovered that there was far too much information in the four exams to create a single volume—that would have resulted in a book that was neither portable nor quick as a reference. So, I jokingly suggested that they let me author four books—one for each exam. Well, I guess you have to be careful what you wish for, because Cisco Press readily agreed. They were so excited about the idea that they offered to *cut* the proposed writing time by a few months to get these books to market faster. How nice of them, don't you think?

This book is the first in a four-volume set that attempts to summarize the commands and concepts that you need to pass one of the CCNP certification exams—in this case, the Building Scalable Cisco Internetworks exam (642-901). This book follows the format of my previous books, which are in fact a cleaned-up version of my own personal engineering journal. I have long been a fan of what I call the "Engineering Journal"—a small notebook that can be carried around that contains little nuggets of information—commands that you forget; the IP addressing scheme of some remote part of the network; little reminders about how to do something you only have to do once or twice a year but is vital to the integrity and maintenance of your network. This journal has been a constant companion by my side for the past eight years; I only teach some of these concepts every second or third year, so I constantly need to refresh commands and concepts and learn new commands and ideas as they are released by Cisco. With the creation of two brand new CCNP exams, the amount of new information out there is growing on an almost daily basis. There is always a new white paper to read, a new Webinar to view, another slideshow from a Networkers session that I didn't get to. My journals are the best way for me to review because they are written in my own words, words that I can understand. At least, I better understand them, because if I didn't, I have only myself to blame.

To make this guide a more realistic one for you to use, the folks at Cisco Press have decided to continue with my request for an appendix of blank pages—pages that are for you to put your own personal touches—your own configurations, commands that are not in this book but are needed in your world. That way, this book will look less like my journal and more like your own.

I hope that you learn as much from reading this guide as I did when I wrote it.

Networking Devices Used in the Preparation of This Book

To verify the commands in this book, I had to try them out on a few different devices. The following is a list of the equipment I used in the writing of this book:

- C1720 router running Cisco IOS Software Release 12.0(1)XA3, with a fixed Fast Ethernet interface, and a WIC-2A/S serial interface card

- C2620 router running Cisco IOS Software Release 12.3(7)T, with a fixed Fast Ethernet interface, a WIC-2A/S serial interface card, and an NM-1E Ethernet interface

- C2811 ISR bundle with PVDM2, CMME, a WIC-2T, FXS and FXO VICs, running 12.4(3g) IOS

- WS-C3550-24-EMI Catalyst switch, running 12.1(9)EA1c IOS

- WS-C2950-12 Catalyst switch, running version C2950-C3.0(5.3)WC(1) Enterprise Edition software

These devices were not running the latest and greatest versions of Cisco IOS Software. Some of it is quite old.

Those of you familiar with Cisco devices will recognize that a majority of these commands work across the entire range of the Cisco product line. These commands are not limited to the platforms and Cisco IOS versions listed. In fact, in most cases these devices are adequate for someone to continue his or her studies into the CCNP level, too.

Who Should Read This Book

This book is for those people preparing for the CCNP BSCI exam, whether through self-study, on-the-job training and practice, study within the Cisco Academy Program, or study through the use of a Cisco Training Partner. There are also some handy hints and tips along the way to make life a bit easier for you in this endeavor. It is small enough that you will find it easy to carry around with you. Big heavy textbooks might look impressive on your bookshelf in your office, but can you really carry them all around with you when you are working in some server room or equipment closet somewhere?

Organization of This Book

This book follows the list of objectives for the CCNP BSCI exam:

- **Chapter 1, "Network Design Requirements"**—An overview of the two different design models from Cisco—the Service-Oriented Network Architecture and the Enterprise Composite Network Model

- **Chapter 2, "EIGRP"**—How to configure, verify, and troubleshoot EIGRP, including topics such as auto-summarization, default networks, authentication, and stub networks

- **Chapter 3, "OSPF"**—How to configure, verify, and troubleshoot OSPF, including topics such as using wildcard masks, router IDs, DR/BDR elections, cost metrics, authentication, timers, default routes, summarization, OSPF and Frame Relay, special area types, and virtual links

- **Chapter 4, "Integrated IS-IS"**—How to configure, verify, and troubleshoot IS-IS, including topics such as OSI addressing, DIS elections, metrics, summarization, default routes, and router types
- **Chapter 5, "Manipulating Routing Updates"**—Including topics such as route redistribution, passive interfaces, route filtering using distribute lists, route maps, administrative distances, floating static routes, recursive lookups, and DHCP on a Cisco IOS router
- **Chapter 6, "BGP"**—How to configure, verify, and troubleshoot BGP, including topics such as loopback addresses, eBGP multihop, autonomous system synchronization, default routes, load balancing, authentication, working with BGP attributes, regular expressions, and route filtering using both ACLs and prefix lists
- **Chapter 7, "Multicast"**—How to configure, verify, and troubleshoot IP multicast, including topics such as multicast address examples, IGMP snooping, CGMP, PIM, Auto-RP, and multicast groups
- **Chapter 8, "IPv6"**—How to configure, verify, and troubleshoot IPv6, including topics such as assigning addresses to interfaces, IPv6 and RIPng, IPv6 and OSPFv3, IPv6 tunnels, static routes, and the ICMP ping utility for IPv6

Did I Miss Anything?

I am always interested to hear how my students, and now readers of my books, do on both vendor exams and future studies. If you would like to contact me and let me know how this book helped you in your certification goals, please do so. Did I miss anything? Let me know. I can't guarantee I'll answer your e-mail message, but I can guarantee that I will read all of them. My e-mail address is ccnpguide@empson.ca.

CHAPTER 1

Network Design Requirements

This chapter provides information concerning the following network design requirement topics:

- Cisco Service-Oriented Network Architecture
- Cisco Enterprise Composite Network Model

No commands are associated with this module of the CCNP Building Scalable Cisco Internetworks (BSCI) course objectives.

Cisco Service-Oriented Network Architecture

Figure 1-1 shows the Cisco Service-Oriented Network Architecture (SONA) framework.

Figure 1-1   Cisco Service-Oriented Network Architecture (SONA) Framework

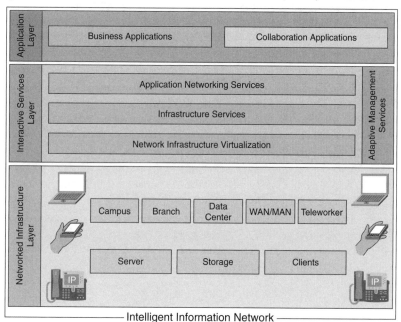

Cisco Enterprise Composite Network Model

Figure 1-2 shows the Cisco Enterprise Composite Network Model.

Figure 1-2 Cisco Enterprise Composite Network Model

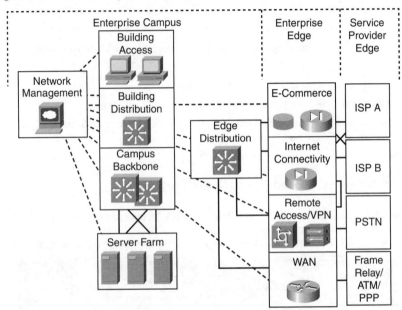

CHAPTER 2

EIGRP

This chapter provides information and commands concerning the following Enhanced Interior Gateway Routing Protocol (EIGRP) topics:

- Configuring EIGRP
- EIGRP auto-summarization
- Injecting a default route into EIGRP: IP default network
- Injecting a default route into EIGRP: Summarize to 0.0.0.0/0
- Load balancing: Variance
- Bandwidth use
- Authentication
- Stub networks
- Verifying EIGRP
- Troubleshooting EIGRP
- Configuration example: EIGRP
- Austin Router
- Houston router

Configuring EIGRP

`Router(config)#router eigrp 100`	Turns on the EIGRP process. 100 is the autonomous system number, which can be a number between 1 and 65,535.
	All routers in the same autonomous system must use the same autonomous system number.
`Router(config-router)#network 10.0.0.0`	Specifies which network to advertise in EIGRP.
`Router(config-if)#bandwidth x`	Sets the bandwith of this interface to x kilobits to allow EIGRP to make a better metric calculation.
	TIP: The **bandwidth** command is used for metric calculations only. It does not change interface performance.
`Router(config-router)#no network 10.0.0.0`	Removes the network from the EIGRP process.
`Router(config)#no router eigrp 100`	Disables routing process 100.

`Router(config-`
`router)#network 10.0.0.0`
`0.255.255.255`
	Identifies which interfaces or networks to include in EIGRP. Interfaces must be configured with addresses that fall within the wildcard mask range of the **network** statement. A network mask can also be used here.

`Router(config-` `router)#metric weights` *tos* *k1 k2 k3 k4 k5*	Changes the default *k* values used in metric calculation. These are the default values: tos=0, k1=1, k2=0, k3=1, k4=0, k5=0

NOTE: *tos* is a reference to the original IGRP intention to have IGRP perform type of service routing. Because this was never adopted into practice, the *tos* field in this command is *always* set to zero.

NOTE: With default settings in place, the metric of EIGRP is reduced to the slowest bandwidth plus the sum of all the delays of the exit interfaces from the local router to the destination network.

TIP: For two routers to form a neighbor relationship in EIGRP, the *k* values *must* match.

CAUTION: Unless you are *very* familiar with what is occurring in your network, it is recommended that you *do not* change the *k* values.

EIGRP Auto-Summarization

`Router(config-router)#auto-` `summary`	Enables auto-summarization for the EIGRP process.
	NOTE: The default behavior of auto-summarized changed from enabled to disabled was introduced in Cisco IOS Software Release 12.2(8)T.
`Router(config-router)#no auto-` `summary`	Turns off the auto-summarization feature.
	NOTE: The behavior of the **auto-summary** command is disabled by default, beginning in Cisco IOS Software Release 12.2(8)T. This means that Cisco IOS Software will now send subprefix routing information across classful network boundaries.

`Router(config)#int fa 0/0`	Enters interface configuration mode.
`Router(config-if)#ip summary-address eigrp 100 10.10.0.0 255.255.0.0 75`	Enables manual summarization for EIGRP autonomous system 100 on this specific interface for the given address and mask. An administrative distance of 75 is assigned to this summary route.
	NOTE: The *administrative-distance* argument is optional in this command. Without it, an administrative distance of 5 is automatically applied to the summary route.

CAUTION: EIGRP automatically summarizes networks at the classful boundary. A poorly designed network with discontiguous subnets could have problems with connectivity if the summarization feature is left on. For instance, you could have two routers advertise the same network—172.16.0.0/16—when in fact they wanted to advertise two different networks—172.16.10.0/24 and 172.16.20.0/24.

Recommended practice is that you turn off automatic summarization if necessary, use the **ip summary-address** command, and summarize manually what you need to.

Injecting a Default Route into EIGRP: Redistribution of a Static Route

`Router(config)#ip route 0.0.0.0 0.0.0.0 s0/0`	Creates a static default route to send all traffic with a destination network not in the routing table out interface serial 0/0.
	NOTE: Adding a static route to an Ethernet or other broadcast interface (for example, ip route 0.0.0.0 0.0.0.0 Ethernet 1/2) will cause the route to be inserted into the routing table only when the interface is up. This configuration is not generally recommended.
`Router(config)#router eigrp 100`	Creates EIGRP routing process 100.
`Router(config-router)#redistribute static`	Static routes on this router will be exchanged with neighbor routers in EIGRP.

NOTE: Use this method when you want to draw all traffic to unknown destinations to a default route at the core of the network.

NOTE: This method is effective for advertising connections to the Internet, but it will redistribute all static routes into EIGRP.

Injecting a Default Route into EIGRP: IP Default Network

`Router(config)#router eigrp 100`	Creates EIGRP routing process 100.
`Router(config-router)#network 192.168.100.0`	Specifies which network to advertise in EIGRP.
`Router(config-router)#exit`	Returns to global configuration mode.
`Router(config)#ip route 0.0.0.0 0.0.0.0 192.168.100.5`	Creates a static default route to send all traffic with a destination network not in the routing table to next hop address 192.168.100.5.
`Router(config)#ip default-network 192.168.100.0`	Defines a route to the 192.168.100.0 network as a candidate default route.

NOTE: For EIGRP to propagate the route, the network specified by the **ip default-network** command must be known to EIGRP. This means the network must be an EIGRP-derived network in the routing table, or the static route used to generate the route to the network must be redistributed into EIGRP, or advertised into these protocols using the **network** command.

TIP: In a complex topology, many networks can be identified as candidate defaults. Without any dynamic protocols running, you can configure your router to choose from a number of candidate default routes based on whether the routing table has routes to networks other than 0.0.0.0/0. The **ip default-network** command enables you to configure robustness into the selection of a gateway of last resort. Rather than configuring static routes to specific next hops, you can have the router choose a default route to a particular network by checking in the routing table.

Injecting a Default Route into EIGRP: Summarize to 0.0.0.0/0

`Router(config)#router eigrp 100`	Creates EIGRP routing process 100.
`Router(config-router)#network 192.168.100.0`	Specifies which network to advertise in EIGRP.
`Router(config-router)#exit`	Returns to global configuration mode.
`Router(config)#interface serial 0/0`	Enters interface configuration mode.
`Router(config-if)#ip address 192.168.100.1 255.255.255.0`	Assigns the IP address and subnet mask to the interface.
`Router(config-if)#ip summary-address eigrp 100 0.0.0.0 0.0.0.0 75`	Enables manual summarization for EIGRP autonomous system 100 on this specific interface for the given address and mask. An optional administrative distance of 75 is assigned to this summary route.

NOTE: Summarizing to a default route is effective only when you want to provide remote sites with a default route, and not propagate the default route toward the core of your network.

NOTE: Because summaries are configured per interface, you don't need to worry about using distribute lists or other mechanisms to prevent the default route from being propagated toward the core of your network.

Load Balancing: Variance

`Router(config)#router eigrp 100`	Creates routing process 100.
`Router(config-router)#network 10.0.0.0`	Specifies which network to advertise in EIGRP.
`Router(config-router)#variance n`	Instructs the router to include routes with a metric less than or equal to n times the minimum metric route for that destination, where n is the number specified by the variance command.

NOTE: If a path isn't a feasible successor, it isn't used in load balancing.

NOTE: EIGRP supports up to six unequal-cost paths.

Bandwidth Use

`Router(config)#interface serial 0/0`	Enters interface configuration mode.
`Router(config-if)#bandwidth 256`	Sets the bandwidth of this interface to 256 kilobits to allow EIGRP to make a better metric calculation.
`Router(config-if)#ip bandwidth-percent eigrp 50 100`	Configures the percentage of bandwidth that may be used by EIGRP on an interface.
	50 is the EIGRP autonomous system number.
	100 is the percentage value.
	100% * 256 = 256 kbps.

NOTE: By default, EIGRP is set to use only up to 50 percent of the bandwidth of an interface to exchange routing information. Values greater than 100 percent can be configured. This configuration option might prove useful if the bandwidth is set artificially low for other reasons, such as manipulation of the routing metric or to accommodate an oversubscribed multipoint Frame Relay configuration.

NOTE: The **ip bandwidth-percent** command relies on the value set by the **bandwidth** command.

Authentication

`Router(config)#interface serial 0/0`	Enters interface configuration mode.
`Router(config-if)#ip authentication mode eigrp 100 md5`	Enables Message Digest 5 (MD5) authentication in EIGRP packets over the interface.
`Router(config-if)#ip authentication key-chain eigrp 100 romeo`	Enables authentication of EIGRP packets. **romeo** is the name of the key chain.

`Router(config-if)#exit`	Returns to global configuration mode.
`Router(config)#key chain romeo`	Identifies a key chain. Name must match the name configured in interface configuration mode above.
`Router(config-keychain)#key 1`	Identifies the key number.
	NOTE: The range of keys is from 0 to 2147483647. The key identification numbers do not need to be consecutive. There must be at least 1 key defined on a key chain.
`Router(config-keychain-key)#key-string shakespeare`	Identifies the key string.
	NOTE: The string can contain from 1 to 80 uppercase and lowercase alphanumeric characters, except that the first character cannot be a number.
`Router(config-keychain-key)#accept-lifetime start-time {infinite I end-time I duration seconds}`	Optionally specifies the period during which the key can be received.
	NOTE: The default start time and the earliest acceptable date is January 1, 1993. The default end time is an infinite time period.
`Router(config-keychain-key)#send-lifetime start-time {infinite I end-time I duration seconds}`	Optionally specifies the period during which the key can be sent.
	NOTE: The default start time and the earliest acceptable date is January 1, 1993. The default end time is an infinite period.

NOTE: For the start time and the end time to have relevance, ensure that the router knows the correct time. Recommended practice dictates that you run Network Time Protocol (NTP) or some other time-synchronization method if you intend to set lifetimes on keys.

Stub Networks

`Router(config)#router eigrp 100`	Creates routing process 100.
`Router(config-router)#eigrp stub`	Router will send updates containing its connected and summary routes only.
	NOTE: Only the stub router needs to have the **eigrp stub** command enabled.
`Router(config-router)#eigrp stub connected`	Permits the EIGRP Stub Routing feature to send only connected routes.
	NOTE: If the connected routes are not covered by a **network** statement, it might be necessary to redistribute connected routes with the **redistribute connected** command.
	TIP: The **connected** option is enabled by default.
`Router(config-router)#eigrp stub static`	Permits the EIGRP Stub Routing feature to send static routes.
	NOTE: Without this option, EIGRP will not send static routes, including internal static routes that normally would be automatically redistributed. It will still be necessary to redistribute static routes with the **redistribute static** command.
`Router(config-router)#eigrp stub summary`	Permits the EIGRP Stub Routing feature to send summary routes.
	NOTE: Summary routes can be created manually, or through automatic summarization at a major network boundary if the **auto-summary** command is enabled.
	TIP: The **summary** option is enabled by default.
`Router(config-router)#eigrp stub receive-only`	Restricts the router from sharing any of its routes with any other router in that EIGRP autonomous system.

NOTE: You can use the three optional arguments (**connected, static**, and **summary**) as part of the same command on a single line: Router(config-router)#**eigrp stub connected static summary**. You cannot use the keyword **receive-only** with any other option because it prevents any type of route from being sent.

TIP: If you use any of the three keywords (**connected, static, summary**) individually with the **eigrp stub** command, connected and summary routes will not be sent automatically. For example, if you use the command that follows, summary routes will not be permitted:

```
Router(config-router)#eigrp stub connected static
```

Verifying EIGRP

Router#`show ip eigrp neighbors`	Displays the neighbor table.
Router#`show ip eigrp neighbors detail`	Displays a detailed neighbor table.
	TIP: The **show ip eigrp neighbors detail** command will verify whether a neighbor is configured as a stub router.
Router#`show ip eigrp interfaces`	Shows info for each interface.
Router#`show ip eigrp int s 0/0`	Shows info for specific interface.
Router#`show ip eigrp int 100`	Shows info for interfaces running process 100.
Router#`show ip eigrp topology`	Displays topology table.
	TIP: The **show ip eigrp topology** command shows you where your feasible successors are.
Router#`show ip eigrp traffic`	Shows the number and type of packets sent and received.
Router#`show ip route eigrp`	Shows a routing table with only EIGRP entries.

Troubleshooting EIGRP

Router#**debug eigrp fsm**	Displays events/actions related to EIGRP feasible successor metrics (FSM).
Router#**debug eigrp packet**	Displays events/actions related to EIGRP packets.
Router#**debug eigrp neighbor**	Displays events/actions related to your EIGRP neighbors.
Router#**debug ip eigrp neighbor**	Displays events/actions related to your EIGRP neighbors.
Router#**debug ip eigrp notifications**	Displays EIGRP event notifications.

Configuration Example: EIGRP

Figure 2-1 shows the network topology for the configuration that follows, which shows how to configure EIGRP using the commands covered in this chapter.

Figure 2-1   Network Topology for EIGRP Configuration

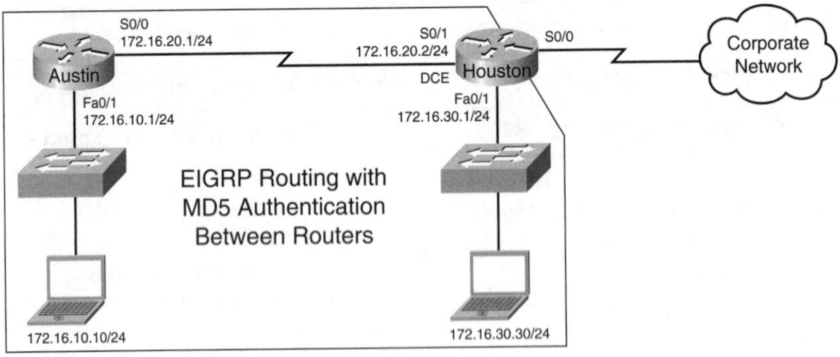

Austin Router

Austin>**en**	
Austin#**config t**	
Austin(config)#**interface s 0/0**	Enters interface configuration mode.
Austin(config-if)#**ip address 172.16.20.1 255.255.255.0**	Assigns the IP address and mask.

`Austin(config-if)#ip authentication mode eigrp 100 md5`	Enables MD5 authentication in EIGRP packets.
`Austin(config-if)#ip authentication key-chain eigrp 100 susannah`	Enables authentication of EIGRP packets. **susannah** is the name of the key chain.
`Austin(config-if)#no shut`	Turns on the interface.
`Austin(config-if)#interface fa0/1`	Enters interface configuration mode.
`Austin(config-if)#ip address 172.16.10.1 255.255.255.0`	Assigns the IP address and mask.
`Austin(config-if)#no shut`	Turns on the interface.
`Austin(config-if)#router eigrp 100`	Enables EIGRP routing.
`Austin(config-router)#no auto-summary`	Disables auto-summarization.
`Austin(config-router)#eigrp log-neighbor-changes`	Changes with neighbors will be displayed.
`Austin(config-router)#network 172.16.0.0`	Advertises directly connected networks (classful address only).
`Austin(config-router)#eigrp stub`	Declares this router to be a stub router.
`Austin(config-router)#key chain susannah`	Identifies a key chain name, which must match the name configured in interface configuration mode.
`Austin(config-keychain)#key 1`	Identifies the key number.
`Austin(config-keychain-key)#key-string tower`	Identifies the key string.
`Austin(config-keychain-key)#accept-lifetime 06:30:00 Apr 19 2007 infinite`	Specifies the period during which the key can be received.
`Austin(config-keychain-key)#send-lifetime 06:30:00 Apr 19 2007 09:45:00 Apr 19 2007`	Specifies the period during which the key can be sent.
`Austin(config-keychain-key)#exit`	Returns to global configuration mode.
`Austin(config)#exit`	
`Austin#copy run start`	

Houston Router

Houston>**en**	
Houston#**config t**	
Houston(config)#**interface s 0/1**	Enters interface configuration mode.
Houston(config-if)#**ip address 172.16.20.2 255.255.255.0**	Assigns the IP address and mask.
Houston(config-if)#**ip authentication mode eigrp 100 md5**	Enables MD5 authentication in EIGRP packets.
Houston(config-if)#**ip authentication key-chain eigrp 100 eddie**	Enables authentication of EIGRP packets. **eddie** is the name of the key chain.
Houston(config-if)#**clock rate 56000**	Sets the clock rate.
Houston(config-if)#**no shut**	Turns on the interface.
Houston(config-if)#**interface fa0/1**	Enters the interface configuration mode.
Houston(config-if)#**ip address 172.16.30.1 255.255.255.0**	Assigns the IP address and mask.
Houston(config-if)#**no shut**	Turns on the interface.
Houston(config-if)#**router eigrp 100**	Enables EIGRP routing.
Houston(config-router)#**no auto-summary**	Disables auto-summarization.
Houston(config-router)#**eigrp log-neighbor-changes**	Changes with neighbors will be displayed.
Houston(config-router)#**network 172.16.0.0**	Advertises directly connected networks (classful address only).
Houston(config-router)#**key chain eddie**	Identifies a key chain name, which must match the name configured in interface configuration mode.
Houston(config-keychain)#**key 1**	Identifies the key number.
Houston(config-keychain-key)#**key-string tower**	Identifies the key string.

Houston(config-keychain-key)#**accept-lifetime 06:30:00 Apr 19 2007 infinite**	Specifies the period during which the key can be received.
Houston(config-keychain-key)#**send-lifetime 06:30:00 Apr 19 2007 09:45:00 Apr 19 2007**	Specifies the period during which the key can be sent.
Houston(config-keychain-key)#**exit**	Returns to global configuration mode.
Houston(config)#**exit**	
Houston#**copy run start**	

OSPF

This chapter provides information and commands concerning the following Open Shortest Path First (OSPF) topics:

- Configuring OSPF: Mandatory commands
- Using wildcard masks with OSPF areas
- Configuring OSPF: Optional commands
  - Loopback interfaces
  - Router ID
  - DR/BDR elections
  - Modifying cost metrics
  - OSPF auto-cost reference-bandwidth
  - Authentication: Simple
  - Authentication: Using MD5 encryption
  - Timers
  - Configuring multi-area OSPF
  - Propagating a default route
  - OSPF and NBMA networks
  - OSPF special area types
  - Virtual Links: Configuration example
  - Route summarization
- Verifying OSPF configuration
- Troubleshooting OSPF
- Configuration example: OSPF and NBMA networks
- Configuration example: OSPF and broadcast networks
- Configuration example: OSPF and point-to-point networks
- Configuration example: OSPF and point-to-point networks using subinterfaces

Configuring OSPF: Mandatory Commands

Router(config)#**router ospf 123**	Starts OSPF process 123. The process ID is any positive integer value between 1 and 65,535. The process ID *is not related to* the OSPF area. The process ID merely distinguishes one process from another within the device.

`Router(config-router)#network` `172.16.10.0 0.0.0.255 area 0`	OSPF advertises interfaces, not networks. Uses the wildcard mask to determine which interfaces to advertise. Read this line to say "Any interface with an address of 172.16.10.x is to be put into Area 0."
	NOTE: The process ID number of one router does not have to match the process ID of any other router. Unlike Enhanced Interior Gateway Routing Protocol (EIGRP), matching this number across all routers does *not* ensure that network adjacencies will form.
`Router(config-router)#log-` `adjacency-changes detail`	Configures the router to send a syslog message when there is a change of state between OSPF neighbors.
	TIP: Although the **log-adjacency-changes** command is on by default, only up/down events are reported unless you use the **detail** keyword.

Using Wildcard Masks with OSPF Areas

When compared to an IP address, a wildcard mask will identify what addresses get matched for placement into an area:

- A 0 (zero) in a wildcard mask means to check the corresponding bit in the address for an exact match.
- A 1 (one) in a wildcard mask means to ignore the corresponding bit in the address—can be either 1 or 0.

Example 1: 172.16.0.0 0.0.255.255

$$
\begin{aligned}
172.16.0.0 &= 10101100.00010000.00000000.00000000 \\
0.0.255.255 &= 00000000.00000000.11111111.11111111 \\
\hline
\text{result} &= 10101100.00010000.xxxxxxxx.xxxxxxxx
\end{aligned}
$$

172.16.*x.x* (Anything between 172.16.0.0 and 172.16.255.255 will match the example statement.)

TIP: An octet of all zeros means that the octet has to match the address exactly. An octet of all ones means that the octet can be ignored.

Example 2: 172.16.8.0 0.0.7.255

$$172.168.8.0 = 10101100.00010000.00001000.00000000$$
$$0.0.0.7.255 = \underline{00000000.00000000.00000111.11111111}$$
$$\text{result} = 10101100.00010000.00001xxx.xxxxxxxx$$
$$00001xxx = 00001000 \text{ to } 00001111 = 8 - 15$$
$$xxxxxxxx = 00000000 \text{ to } 11111111 = 0 - 255$$

Anything between 172.16.8.0 and 172.16.15.255 will match the example statement.

`Router(config-router)#network` `172.16.10.1 0.0.0.0 area 0`	Read this line to say "Any interface with an exact address of 172.16.10.1 is to be put into Area 0."
`Router(config-router)#network` `172.16.10.0 0.0.255.255 area 0`	Read this line to say "Any interface with an address of 172.16.x.x is to be put into Area 0."
`Router(config-router)#network 0.0.0.0` `255.255.255.255 area 0`	Read this line to say "Any interface with any address is to be put into Area 0."

Configuring OSPF: Optional Commands

The following commands, although not mandatory, enable you to have a more controlled and efficient deployment of OSPF in your network.

Loopback Interfaces

`Router(config)#interface lo0`	Creates a virtual interface named Loopback 0, and then moves the router to interface configuration mode.
`Router(config-if)#ip address` `192.168.100.1 255.255.255.255`	Assigns the IP address to the interface.
	NOTE: Loopback interfaces are always "up and up" and do not go down unless manually shut down. This makes loopback interfaces great for use as an OSPF router ID.

Router ID

`Router(config)#`**`router ospf 1`**	Starts OSPF process 1.
`Router(config-router)#`**`router-id`** **`10.1.1.1`**	Sets the router ID to 10.1.1.1. If this command is used on an OSPF router process that is already active (has neighbors), the new router ID is used at the next reload or at a manual OSPF process restart.
`Router(config-router)#`**`no`** **`router-id 10.1.1.1`**	Removes the static router ID from the configuration. If this command is used on an OSPF router process that is already active (has neighbors), the old router ID behavior is used at the next reload or at a manual OSPF process restart.

DR/BDR Elections

`Router(config)#`**`interface`** **`serial 0/0`**	Changes the router to interface configuration mode.
`Router(config-if)#`**`ip ospf`** **`priority 50`**	Changes the OSPF interface priority to 50.
	NOTE: The assigned priority can be between 0 and 255. A priority of 0 makes the router ineligible to become a designated router (DR) or backup designated router (BDR). The highest priority wins the election. A priority of 255 guarantees a tie in the election. If all routers have the same priority, regardless of the priority number, they tie. Ties are broken by the highest router ID.

Modifying Cost Metrics

`Router(config)#`**`interface`** **`serial 0/0`**	Changes the router to interface configuration mode.
`Router(config-if)#`**`bandwidth 128`**	If you change the bandwidth, OSPF will recalculate the cost of the link.
Or	
`Router(config-if)#`**`ip ospf cost`** **`1564`**	Changes the cost to a value of 1564.

	NOTE: The cost of a link is determined by dividing the reference bandwidth by the interface bandwidth.
	The bandwidth of the interface is a number between 1 and 10,000,000. The unit of measurement is kilobits.
	The cost is a number between 1 and 65,535. The cost has no unit of measurement—it is just a number.

OSPF auto-cost reference-bandwidth

`Router(config)#`**`router ospf 1`**	Starts OSPF process 1.
`Router(config-router)#`**`auto-cost`** **`reference-bandwidth 1000`**	Changes the reference bandwidth that OSPF uses to calculate the cost of an interface.
	NOTE: The range of the reference bandwidth is 1 to 4,294,967. The default is 100. The unit of measurement is Mbps.
	NOTE: The value set by the **ip ospf cost** command overrides the cost resulting from the **auto-cost** command.
	TIP: If you use the command **auto-cost reference-bandwidth** *reference-bandwidth*, configure all the routers to use the same value. Failure to do so will result in routers using a different reference cost to calculate the shortest path, resulting in potential suboptimum routing paths.

Authentication: Simple

`Router(config)#`**`router ospf 1`**	Starts OSPF process 1.
`Router(config-router)#`**`area 0`** **`authentication`**	Enables simple authentication; password will be sent in clear text.
`Router(config-router)#`**`exit`**	Returns to global configuration mode.
`Router(config)#`**`interface`** **`fastethernet 0/0`**	Moves to interface configuration mode.

`Router(config-if)#ip ospf` `authentication-key fred`	Sets key (password) to fred.
	NOTE: The password can be any continuous string of characters that can be entered from the keyboard, up to 8 bytes in length. To be able to exchange OSPF information, all neighboring routers on the same network must have the same password.

Authentication: Using MD5 Encryption

`Router(config)#`**`router ospf 1`**	Starts OSPF process 1.
`Router(config-router)#`**`area 0`** **`authentication message-digest`**	Enables authentication with MD5 password encryption.
`Router(config-router)#`**`exit`**	Returns to global configuration mode.
`Router(config)#`**`interface`** **`fastethernet 0/0`**	Moves to interface configuration mode.
Router(config-if)#**ip ospf message-digest-key 1 md5 fred**	1 is the *key-id*. This value must be the same as that of your neighboring router. **md5** indicates that the MD5 hash algorithm will be used. **fred** is the key (password) and must be the same as that of your neighboring router.
	NOTE: If the service password-encryption command is not used when implementing OSPF MD5 authentication, the MD5 secret will be stored as plain text in NVRAM.

Timers

`Router(config-if)#`**`ip ospf hello-`**`interval timer 20`	Changes the Hello Interval timer to 20 seconds.
`Router(config-if)#`**`ip ospf dead-`**`interval 80`	Changes the Dead Interval timer to 80 seconds.
	NOTE: Hello and Dead Interval timers must match for routers to become neighbors.

Configuring Multi-Area OSPF

`Router(config)#router ospf 1`	Starts OSPF process 1.
`Router(config-router)#network 172.16.10.0 0.0.0.255 area 0`	Read this line to say "Any interface with an address of 172.16.10.*x* is to be put into area 0."
`Router(config-router)#network 10.10.10.1 0.0.0.0 area 51`	Read this line to say "Any interface with an exact address of 10.10.10.1 is to be put into area 51."

Propagating a Default Route

`Router(config)#ip route 0.0.0.0 0.0.0.0 s0/0`	Creates a default route.
`Router(config)#router ospf 1`	Starts OSPF process 1.
`Router(config-router)#default-information originate`	Sets the default route to be propagated to all OSPF routers.
`Router(config-router)#default-information originate always`	The always option will propagate a default "quad-zero" route even if one is not configured on this router.
	NOTE: The **default-information originate** command or the **default-information originate always** command is usually only to be configured on your "entrance" or "gateway" router, the router that connects your network to the outside world—the Autonomous System Boundary Router (ASBR).

OSPF and NBMA Networks

OSPF it not well suited for nonbroadcast multiaccess (NBMA) networks such as Frame Relay or ATM. The term *multiaccess* means that an NBMA cloud is seen as a single network that has multiple devices attached to it, much like an Ethernet network. However, the *nonbroadcast* part of NBMA means that a packet sent into this network might not be seen by all other routers, which differs from broadcast technologies such as Ethernet. OSPF will want to elect a DR and BDR because an NBMA network is multiaccess; however, because the network is also nonbroadcast, there is no guarantee that all OSPF packets, such as Hello packets, would be received by other routers. This could affect the election of the DR because not all routers would know about all the other routers. The following section lists some possible solutions to dealing with OSPF in NBMA networks.

Full-Mesh Frame Relay: NBMA on Physical Interfaces

`Router(config)#router ospf 1`	Starts OSPF process 1.
`Router(config-router)#network 10.1.1.0 0.0.0.255 area 0`	Read this line to say "Any interface with an address of 10.1.1.x is to be put into area 0."
`Router(config-router)#neighbor 10.1.1.2`	Manually identifies this router's neighbor at IP address 10.1.1.2.
`Router(config-router)#neighbor 10.1.1.3 priority 15`	Manually identifies this router's neighbor at IP address 10.1.1.3 and assigns a priority value of 15 to determine the DR.
`Router(config-router)#exit`	Returns to global configuration mode.
`Router(config)#interface serial 0/0`	Moves to interface configuration mode.
`Router(config-if)#encapsulation frame-relay`	Enables Frame Relay on this interface.
`Router(config-if)#ip address 10.1.1.1 255.255.255.0`	Assigns an IP address and netmask to this interface.
`Router(config-if)#frame-relay map ip 10.1.1.2 100`	Maps the remote IP address 10.1.1.2 to data-link connection identifier (DLCI) 100.
`Router(config-if)#frame-relay map ip 10.1.1.3 200`	Maps the remote IP address 10.1.1.3 to DLCI 200.
	NOTE: Using the **neighbor** command will allow for an OSPF router to exchange routing information without multicasts and instead use unicasts to the manually entered neighbor IP address.
	NOTE: Prior to Cisco IOS Software Release 12.0, the neighbor command applied to NBMA networks only. With Release 12.0, the neighbor command applies to NBMA networks and point-to-multipoint networks.

Full-Mesh Frame Relay: Broadcast on Physical Interfaces

`Router(config)#interface serial 0/0`	Moves to interface configuration mode.
`Router(config-if)#encapsulation frame-relay`	Enables Frame Relay on this interface.
`Router(config-if)#ip address 10.1.1.1 255.255.255.0`	Assigns an IP address and netmask to this interface.
`Router(config-if)#ip ospf network broadcast`	Changes the network type to *broadcast* instead of *NBMA*.
`Router(config-if)#ip ospf priority 15`	Changes the OSPF interface priority to 15.
`Router(config-if)#frame-relay map ip 10.1.1.2 100 broadcast`	Maps the remote IP address 10.1.1.2 to DLCI 100. Broadcast and multicast addresses will now be forwarded.
`Router(config-if)#frame-relay map ip 10.1.1.3 200 broadcast`	Maps the remote IP address 10.1.1.3 to DLCI 200. Broadcast and multicast addresses will now be forwarded.
`Router(config-if)#no shutdown`	Enables the interface.
`Router(config)#router ospf 1`	Starts OSPF process 1.
`Router(config-router)#network 10.1.1.0 0.0.0.255 area 0`	Read this line to say "Any interface with an address of 10.1.1.*x* is to be put into area 0."
	NOTE: If you want to influence the DR election, another option is to create a fully meshed topology— every router has a permanent virtual circuit (PVC) to every other router. This is efficient in terms of NBMA network designs. However, this is also a costly solution—for *n* routers, you need $n(n-1)/2$ PVCs. A 5-router full mesh would mean 10 PVCs are needed; 20 routers would mean 190 PVCs are needed.

Full Mesh Frame Relay: Point-to-Multipoint Networks

`Router(config)#interface serial 0/0`	Moves to interface configuration mode.
`Router(config-if)#encapsulation frame-relay`	Enables Frame Relay on this interface.
`Router(config-if)#ip address 10.1.1.1 255.255.255.0`	Assigns an IP address and netmask to this interface.
`Router(config-if)#ip ospf network point-to-multipoint`	Network is changed to a point-to-multipoint network.
`Router(config-if)#exit`	Returns to global configuration mode.
`Router(config)#router ospf 1`	Starts OSPF process 1.
`Router(config-router)#network 10.1.1.0 0.0.0.255 area 0`	Read this line to say "Any interface with an address of 10.1.1.x is to be put into area 0."
	NOTE: In this example, Inverse Address Resolution Protocol (ARP) is used to dynamically map IP addresses to DLCIs. Static maps could have been used, if desired.
	NOTE: Point-to-multipoint networks treat PVCs as a collection of point-to-point links rather than a multiaccess network. No DR/BDR election will take place.
	NOTE: Point-to-multipoint networks might be your only alternative to broadcast networks in a multivendor environment.

Full-Mesh Frame Relay: Point-to-Point Networks with Subinterfaces

`Router(config)#interface serial 0/0`	Moves to interface configuration mode.
`Router(config-if)#encapsulation frame-relay`	Enables Frame Relay on this interface.
`Router(config-if)#no shutdown`	Enables the interface.
`Router(config-if)#int s0/0.300 point-to-point`	Creates subinterface 300 and makes it a point-to-point network.

Router(config-subif)#**ip address 192.168.1.1 255.255.255.252**	Assigns an IP address and netmask.
Router(config-subif)#**frame-relay interface-dlci 300**	Assigns DLCI 300 to the subinterface.
Router(config-subif)#**int s0/0.400 point-to-point**	Creates subinterface 400 and makes it a point-to-point network.
Router(config-subif)#**ip address 192.168.1.5 255.255.255.252**	Assigns an IP address and netmask.
Router(config-subif)#**frame-relay interface-dlci 400**	Assigns DLCI 400 to the subinterface.
Router(config-subif)#**exit**	Returns to global configuration mode.
Router(config-if)#**exit**	
Router(config)#**router ospf 1**	Starts OSPF process 1.
Router(config-router)#**network 192.168.1.0 0.0.0.255 area 0**	Read this line to say "Any interface with an address of 192.168.1.x is to be put into area 0."
	NOTE: Point-to-point subinterfaces allow each PVC to be configured as a separate subnet. No DR/BDR election will take place.
	NOTE: The use of subinterfaces increases the amount of memory used on the router.

OSPF Special Area Types

This section covers four different special areas with respect to OSPF:

- Stub areas
- Totally stubby areas
- Not so stubby areas (NSSA) stub area
- NSSA totally stubby areas

Stub Areas

ABR(config)#**router ospf 1**	Starts OSPF process 1.
ABR(config-router)#**network 172.16.10.0 0.0.0.255 area 0**	Any interface with an address of 172.16.10.x is to be put into area 0.

ABR(config-router)#**network 172.16.20.0 0.0.0.255 area 51**	Any interface with an address of 172.16.20.x is to be put into area 51.
ABR(config-router)#**area 51 stub**	Defines area 51 as a stub area.
Internal(config)#**router ospf 1**	Starts OSPF process 1.
Internal(config-router)#**network 172.16.20.0 0.0.0.255 area 51**	Any interface with an address of 172.16.20.x is to be put into area 51.
Internal(config-router)#**area 51 stub**	Defines area 51 as a stub area.
	NOTE: All routers in the stub area must be configured with the area *x* stub command, including the Area Border Router (ABR).

Totally Stubby Areas

ABR(config)#**router ospf 1**	Starts OSPF process 1.
ABR(config-router)#**network 172.16.10.0 0.0.0.255 area 0**	Any interface with an address of 172.16.10.x is to be put into area 0.
ABR(config-router)#**network 172.16.20.0 0.0.0.255 area 51**	Any interface with an address of 172.16.20.x is to be put into area 51.
ABR(config-router)#**area 51 stub no-summary**	Defines area 51 as a totally stubby area.
Internal(config)#**router ospf 1**	Starts OSPF process 1.
Internal(config-router)#**network 172.16.20.0 0.0.0.255 area 51**	Any interface with an address of 172.16.20.x is to be put into area 51.
Internal(config-router)#**area 51 stub**	Defines area 51 as a stub area.
	NOTE: Whereas all internal routers in the area are configured with the **area *x* stub** command, the ABR is configured with the **area *x* stub no-summary** command.

Not So Stubby Areas (NSSA) Stub Area

ABR(config)#**router ospf 1**	Starts OSPF process 1.
ABR(config-router)#**network 172.16.10.0 0.0.0.255 area 0**	Any interface with an address of 172.16.10.x is to be put into area 0.
ABR(config-router)#**network 172.16.20.0 0.0.0.255 area 1**	Any interface with an address of 172.16.20.x is to be put into area 1.
ABR(config-router)#**area 1 nssa**	Defines area 1 as a NSSA stub area.
Internal(config)#**router ospf 1**	Starts OSPF process 1.
Internal(config-router)#**network 172.16.20.0 0.0.0.255 area 1**	Any interface with an address of 172.16.20.x is to be put into area 1.
Internal(config-router)#**area 1 nssa**	Defines area 1 as an NSSA stub area.
	NOTE: All routers in the NSSA stub area must be configured with the **area** x **nssa** command.

NSSA Totally Stubby Areas

ABR(config)#**router ospf 1**	Starts OSPF process 1.
ABR(config-router)#**network 172.16.10.0 0.0.0.255 area 0**	Any interface with an address of 172.16.10.x is to be put into area 0.
ABR(config-router)#**network 172.16.20.0 0.0.0.255 area 11**	Any interface with an address of 172.16.20.x is to be put into area 11.
ABR(config-router)#**area 11 nssa no-summary**	Defines area 11 as an NSSA totally stubby area.
Internal(config)#**router ospf 1**	Starts OSPF process 1.
Internal(config-router)#**network 172.16.20.0 0.0.0.255 area 11**	Any interface with an address of 172.16.20.x is to be put into area 11.
Internal(config-router)#**area 11 nssa**	Defines area 11 as an NSSA stub area.
	NOTE: Whereas all internal routers in the area are configured with the **area** x **nssa** command, the ABR is configured with the **area** x **nssa no-summary** command.

Virtual Links: Configuration Example

Figure 3-1 shows the network topology for the configuration that follows, which demonstrates how to create a virtual link.

Figure 3-1   Virtual Areas: OSPF

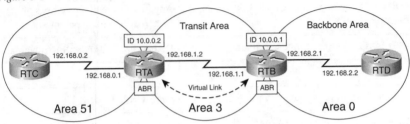

RTA(config)#**router ospf 1**	Starts OSPF process 1.
RTA(config-router)#**router-id 10.0.0.2**	Sets the router ID to 10.0.0.2.
RTA(config-router)#**network 192.168.0.0 0.0.0.255 area 51**	Any interface with an address of 192.168.0.*x* is to be put into area 51.
RTA(config-router)#**network 192.168.1.0 0.0.0.255 area 3**	Any interface with an address of 192.168.1.*x* is to be put into area 3.
RTA(config-router)#**area 3 virtual-link 10.0.0.1**	Creates a virtual link with RTB.
RTB(config)#**router ospf 1**	Starts OSPF process 1.
RTB(config-router)#**router-id 10.0.0.1**	Sets the router ID to 10.0.0.1.
RTB(config-router)#**network 192.168.1.0 0.0.0.255 area 3**	Any interface with an address of 192.168.1.*x* is to be put into area 3.
RTB(config-router)#**network 192.168.2.0 0.0.0.255 area 0**	Any interface with an address of 192.168.2.*x* is to be put into area 0.
RTB(config-router)#**area 3 virtual-link 10.0.0.2**	Creates a virtual link with RTA.
	NOTE: A virtual link has the following two requirements: It must be established between two routers that share a common area and are both ABRs. One of these two routers must be connected to the backbone.

	NOTE: A virtual link is a temporary solution to a topology problem.
	NOTE: A virtual link cannot be configured through stub areas.

Route Summarization

In OSPF, there are two different types of summarization:

- Inter-area route summarization
- External route summarization

The sections that follow provide the commands necessary to configure both types of summarization.

Inter-Area Route Summarization

Router(config)#**router ospf 1**	Starts OSPF process 1.
Router(config-router)#**area 1 range 192.168.64.0 255.255.224.0**	ABR will consolidate routes to this summary address before injecting them into a different area.
	NOTE: This command is to be configured on an ABR only.
	NOTE: By default, ABRs do *not* summarize routes between areas.

External Route Summarization

Router(config)#**router ospf 123**	Starts OSPF process 1.
Router(config-router)#**summary-address 192.168.64.0 255.255.224.0**	Advertises a single route for all the redistributed routes that are covered by a specified network address and netmask.
	NOTE: This command is to be configured on an Autonomous System Border Router (ASBR) only.
	NOTE: By default, ASBRs do *not* summarize routes.

Verifying OSPF Configuration

`Router#show ip protocol`	Displays parameters for all protocols running on the router.
`Router#show ip route`	Displays a complete IP routing table.
`Router#show ip ospf`	Displays basic information about OSPF routing processes.
`Router#show ip ospf interface`	Displays OSPF info as it relates to all interfaces.
`Router#show ip ospf interface fastethernet 0/0`	Displays OSPF information for interface fa0/0.
`Router#show ip ospf border-routers`	Displays border and boundary router information.
`Router#show ip ospf neighbor`	Lists all OSPF neighbors and their states.
`Router#show ip ospf neighbor detail`	Displays a detailed list of neighbors.
`Router#show ip ospf database`	Displays contents of the OSPF database.
`Router#show ip ospf database nssa-external`	Displays NSSA external link states.

Troubleshooting OSPF

`Router#clear ip route *`	Clears the entire routing table, forcing it to rebuild.
`Router#clear ip route a.b.c.d`	Clears a specific route to network a.b.c.d.
`Router#clear ip opsf counters`	Resets OSPF counters.
`Router#clear ip ospf process`	Resets the *entire* OSPF process, forcing OSPF to re-create neighbors, database, and routing table.
`Router#debug ip ospf events`	Displays *all* OSPF events.
`Router#debug ip ospf adjacency`	Displays various OSPF states and DR/BDR election between adjacent routers.
`Router#debug ip ospf packets`	Displays OPSF packets.

Configuration Example: Single-Area OSPF

Figure 3-2 shows the network topology for the configuration that follows, which demonstrates how to configure single-area OSPF using the commands covered in this chapter.

Figure 3-2   Network Topology for Single-Area OSPF ConfigurationI

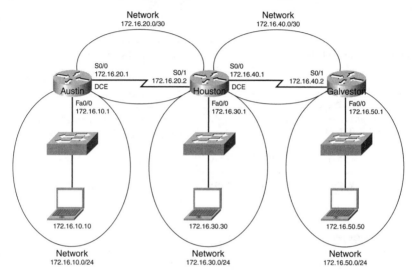

Austin Router

`Router>`**`enable`**	Moves to privileged mode.
`Router#`**`configure terminal`**	Moves to global configuration mode.
`Router(config)#`**`hostname Austin`**	Sets the host name.
`Austin(config)#`**`interface fastethernet 0/0`**	Moves to interface configuration mode.
`Austin(config-if)#`**`ip address 172.16.10.1 255.255.255.0`**	Assigns an IP address and netmask.
`Austin(config-if)#`**`no shutdown`**	Enables the interface.
`Austin(config-if)#`**`interface serial 0/0`**	Moves to interface configuration mode.

Austin(config-if)#`ip address 172.16.20.1 255.255.255.252`	Assigns an IP address and netmask.
Austin(config-if)#`clock rate 56000`	DCE cable plugged in this side.
Austin(config-if)#`no shutdown`	Enables the interface.
Austin(config-if)#`exit`	Returns to global configuration mode.
Austin(config)#`router ospf 1`	Starts OSPF process 1.
Austin(config-router)#`network 172.16.10.0 0.0.0.255 area 0`	Any interface with an address of 172.16.10.*x* is to be put into area 0.
Austin(config-router)#`network 172.16.20.0 0.0.0.255 area 0`	Any interface with an address of 172.16.20.*x* is to be put into area 0.
Austin(config-router)#Ctrl Z	Returns to privileged mode.
Austin#`copy running-config startup-config`	Saves the configuration to NVRAM.

Houston Router

Router>`enable`	Moves to privileged mode.
Router#`configure terminal`	Moves to global configuration mode.
Router(config)#`hostname Houston`	Sets the host name.
Houston(config)#`interface fastethernet 0/0`	Moves to interface configuration mode.
Houston(config-if)#`ip address 172.16.30.1 255.255.255.0`	Assigns an IP address and netmask.
Houston(config-if)#`no shutdown`	Enables the interface.
Houston(config-if)#`interface serial0/0`	Moves to interface configuration mode.
Houston(config-if)#`ip address 172.16.40.1 255.255.255.252`	Assigns an IP address and netmask.
Houston(config-if)#`clock rate 56000`	DCE cable plugged in this side.
Houston(config-if)#`no shutdown`	Enables the interface.

`Houston(config)#interface serial 0/1`	Moves to interface configuration mode.
`Houston(config-if)#ip address` `172.16.20.2 255.255.255.252`	Assigns an IP address and netmask.
`Houston(config-if)#no shutdown`	Enables the interface.
`Houston(config-if)#exit`	Returns to global configuration mode.
`Houston(config)#router ospf 1`	Starts OSPF process 1.
`Houston(config-router)#network` `172.16.0.0 0.0.255.255 area 0`	Any interface with an address of 172.16.$x.x$ is to be put into area 0. One statement will now advertise all three interfaces.
`Houston(config-router)#`Ctrl Z	Returns to privileged mode.
`Houston#copy running-config startup-config`	Saves the configuration to NVRAM.

Galveston Router

`Router>enable`	Moves to privileged mode.
`Router#configure terminal`	Moves to global configuration mode.
`Router(config)#hostname Galveston`	Sets the host name.
`Galveston(config)#interface` `fastethernet 0/0`	Moves to interface configuration mode.
`Galveston(config-if)#ip address` `172.16.50.1 255.255.255.0`	Assigns an IP address and netmask.
`Galveston(config-if)#no shutdown`	Enables the interface.
`Galveston(config-if)#interface serial` `0/1`	Moves to interface configuration mode.
`Galveston(config-if)#ip address` `172.16.40.2 255.255.255.252`	Assigns an IP address and netmask.
`Galveston(config-if)#no shutdown`	Enables the interface.

`Galveston(config-if)#exit`	Returns to global configuration mode.
`Galveston(config)#router ospf 1`	Starts OSPF process 1.
`Galveston(config-router)#network 172.16.40.2 0.0.0.0 area 0`	Any interface with an exact address of 172.16.40.2 is to be put into area 0. This is the most precise way to place an exact address into the OSPF routing process.
`Galveston(config-router)#network 172.16.50.1 0.0.0.0 area 0`	Any interface with an exact address of 172.16.50.2 is to be put into area 0.
`Galveston(config-router)#`Ctrl `z`	Returns to privileged mode.
`Galveston#copy running-config startup-config`	Saves the configuration to NVRAM.

Configuration Example: Multi-Area OSPF

Figure 3-3 shows the network topology for the configuration that follows, which demonstrates how to configure multi-area OSPF using the commands covered in this chapter.

Figure 3-3   Network Topology for Multi-Area OSPF Configuration

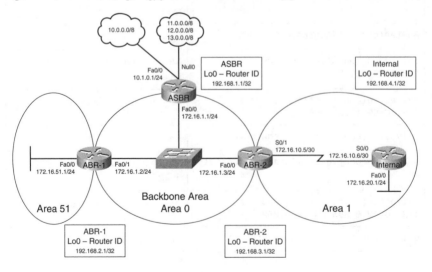

ASBR Router

`Router>`**`enable`**	Moves to privileged mode.
`Router#`**`configure terminal`**	Moves to global configuration mode.
`Router(config)#`**`hostname ASBR`**	Sets the router host name.
`ASBR(config)#`**`interface loopback 0`**	Enters loopback interface mode.
`ASBR(config-if)#`**`ip address 192.168.1.1 255.255.255.255`**	Assigns an IP address and netmask.
`ASBR(config-if)#`**`description Router ID`**	Sets a locally significant description.
`ASBR(config-if)#`**`exit`**	Returns to global configuration mode.
`ASBR(config)#`**`interface fastethernet 0/0`**	Enters interface configuration mode.
`ASBR(config-if)#`**`ip address 172.16.1.1 255.255.255.0`**	Assigns an IP address and netmask.
`ASBR(config-if)#`**`no shutdown`**	Enables the interface.
`ASBR(config-if)#`**`exit`**	Returns to global configuration mode.
`ASBR(config)#`**`ip route 0.0.0.0 0.0.0.0 10.1.0.2 fa0/1`**	Creates default route. Using both an exit interface and next hop address on a Fast Ethernet interface prevents recursive lookups in the routing table.
`ASBR(config)#`**`ip route 11.0.0.0 0.0.0.0 null0`**	Creates a static route to a null interface. In this example, these routes represent a simulated remote destination.
`ASBR(config)#`**`ip route 12.0.0.0 0.0.0.0 null0`**	Creates a static route to a null interface. In this example, these routes represent a simulated remote destination.
`ASBR(config)#`**`ip route 13.0.0.0 0.0.0.0 null0`**	Creates a static route to a null interface. In this example, these routes represent a simulated remote destination.
`ASBR(config)#`**`router ospf 1`**	Starts OPSF process 1.
`ASBR(config-router)#`**`network 172.16.1.0 0.0.0.255 area 0`**	Any interface with an address of 172.16.1.*x* is to be put into area 0.

`ASBR(config-router)#default-information originate`	Sets the default route to be propagated to all OSPF routers.
`ASBR(config-router)#redistribute static`	Redistributes static routes into the OSPF process. This turns the router into an ASBR because static routes are not part of OSPF, and the definition of an ASBR is a router that sits between OSPF and another routing process—in this case, static routing.
`ASBR(config-router)#exit`	Returns to global configuration mode.
`ASBR(config)#exit`	Returns to privileged mode.
`ASBR#copy running-config startup-config`	Saves the configuration to NVRAM.

ABR-1 Router

`Router>en`	Moves to privileged mode.
`Router#configure terminal`	Moves to global configuration mode.
`Router(config)#hostname ABR-1`	Sets the router host name.
`ABR-1(config)#interface loopback 0`	Enters loopback interface mode.
`ABR-1(config-if)#ip address 192.168.2.1 255.255.255.255`	Assigns an IP address and netmask.
`ABR-1(config-if)#description Router ID`	Sets a locally significant description.
`ABR-1(config-if)#exit`	Returns to global configuration mode.
`ABR-1(config)#interface fastethernet 0/1`	Enters interface configuration mode.
`ABR-1(config-if)#ip address 172.16.1.2 255.255.255.0`	Assigns an IP address and netmask.
`ABR-1(config-if)#ip ospf priority 200`	Sets the priority for the DR/BDR election process. This router will win and become the DR.
`ABR-1(config-if)#no shutdown`	Enables the interface.
`ABR-1(config-if)#exit`	Returns to global configuration mode.

`ABR-1(config)#`**`interface`** **`fastethernet 0/0`**	Enters interface configuration mode.
`ABR-1(config-if)#`**`ip address`** **`172.16.51.1 255.255.255.0`**	Assigns an IP address and netmask.
`ABR-1(config-if)#`**`no shutdown`**	Enables the interface.
`ABR-1(config-if)#`**`exit`**	Returns to global configuration mode.
`ABR-1(config)#`**`router ospf 1`**	Starts OPSF process 1.
`ABR-1(config-router)#`**`network`** **`172.16.1.0 0.0.0.255 area 0`**	Any interface with an address of 172.16.1.x is to be put into area 0.
`ABR-1(config-router)#`**`network`** **`172.16.51.1 0.0.0.0 area 51`**	Any interface with an exact address of 172.16.51.1 is to be put into area 51.
`ABR-1(config-router)#`**`exit`**	Returns to global configuration mode.
`ABR-1(config)#`**`exit`**	Returns to privileged mode.
`ABR-1(config)#`**`copy running-config`** **`startup-config`**	Saves the configuration to NVRAM.

ABR-2 Router

`Router>`**`enable`**	Moves to privileged mode.
`Router#`**`configure terminal`**	Moves to global configuration mode.
`Router(config)#`**`hostname ABR-2`**	Sets the router host name.
`ABR-2(config)#`**`interface loopback 0`**	Enters loopback interface mode.
`ABR-2(config-if)#`**`ip address`** **`192.168.3.1 255.255.255.255`**	Assigns an IP address and netmask.
`ABR-2(config-if)#`**`description Router`** **`ID`**	Sets a locally significant description.
`ABR-2(config-if)#`**`exit`**	Returns to global configuration mode.
`ABR-2(config)#`**`interface`** **`fastethernet 0/0`**	Enters interface configuration mode.
`ABR-2(config-if)#`**`ip address`** **`172.16.1.3 255.255.255.0`**	Assigns an IP address and netmask.

`ABR-2(config-if)#ip ospf priority 100`	Sets the priority for the DR/BDR election process. This router will become the BDR to ABR-1's DR.
`ABR-2(config-if)#no shutdown`	Enables the interface.
`ABR-2(config-if)#exit`	Returns to global configuration mode.
`ABR-2(config)#interface serial 0/1`	Enters interface configuration mode.
`ABR-2(config-if)#ip address 172.16.10.5 255.255.255.252`	Assigns an IP address and netmask.
`ABR-2(config-if)#clock rate 56000`	Assigns a clock rate to the interface.
`ABR-2(config-if)#no shutdown`	Enables the interface.
`ABR-2(config-if)#exit`	Returns to global configuration mode.
`ABR-2(config)#router ospf 1`	Starts OPSF process 1.
`ABR-2(config-router)#network 172.16.1.0 0.0.0.255 area 0`	Any interface with an address of 172.16.1.x is to be put into area 0.
`ABR-2(config-router)#network 172.16.10.4 0.0.0.3 area 1`	Any interface with an address of 172.16.10.4–7 is to be put into area 1.
`ABR-2(config-router)#area 1 stub`	Makes area 1 a stub area. LSA type 4 and type 5s are blocked and not sent into area 1. A default route is injected into the stub area, pointing to the ABR.
`ABR-2(config-router)#exit`	Returns to global configuration mode.
`ABR-2(config)#exit`	Returns to privileged mode.
`ABR-2(config)#copy running-config startup-config`	Saves the configuration to NVRAM.

Internal Router

`Router>enable`	Moves to privileged mode.
`Router#configure terminal`	Moves to global configuration mode.
`Router(config)#hostname Internal`	Sets the router host name.
`Internal(config)#interface loopback 0`	Enters loopback interface mode.

`Internal(config-if)#ip address` `192.168.4.1 255.255.255.255`	Assigns an IP address and netmask.
`Internal(config-if)#description` `Router ID`	Sets a locally significant description.
`Internal(config-if)#exit`	Returns to global configuration mode.
`Internal(config)#interface` `fastethernet0/0`	Enters interface configuration mode.
`Internal(config-if)#ip address` `172.16.20.1 255.255.255.0`	Assigns an IP address and netmask.
`Internal(config-if)#no shutdown`	Enables the interface.
`Internal(config-if)#exit`	Returns to global configuration mode.
`Internal(config)#interface serial0/` `0`	Enters interface configuration mode.
`Internal(config-if)#ip address` `172.16.10.6 255.255.255.252`	Assigns an IP address and netmask.
`Internal(config-if)#no shut`	Enables the interface.
`Internal(config-if)#exit`	Returns to global configuration mode.
`Internal(config)#router ospf 1`	Starts OPSF process 1.
`Internal(config-router)#network` `172.16.0.0 0.0.255.255 area 0`	Any interface with an address of 172.16.*x*.*x* is to be put into area 0.
`Internal(config-router)#area 1 stub`	Makes area 1 a stub area.
`Internal(config-router)#exit`	Returns to global configuration mode.
`Internal(config)#exit`	Returns to privileged mode.
`Internal(config)#copy run start`	Saves the configuration to NVRAM.

Configuration Example: OSPF and NBMA Networks

Figure 3-4 shows the network topology for the configuration that follows, which demonstrates how to configure OSPF on an NBMA network using the commands covered in this chapter.

Figure 3-4   Network Topology for OSPF Configuration on an NBMA Network

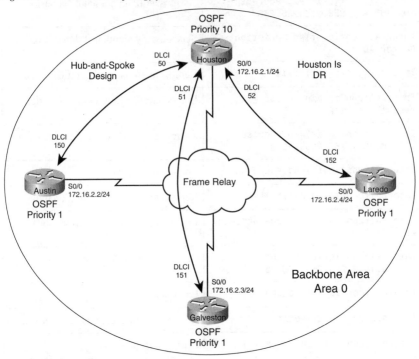

Houston Router

`Router>`**`enable`**	Moves to privileged mode.
`Router#`**`configure terminal`**	Moves to global configuration mode.
`Router(config)#`**`hostname Houston`**	Sets the router host name.
`Houston(config)#`**`interface serial0/0`**	Enters interface configuration mode.
`Houston(config-if)#`**`encapsulation frame-relay`**	Enables Frame Relay encapsulation.
`Houston(config-if)#`**`ip address 172.16.2.1 255.255.255.0`**	Assigns an IP address and netmask.
`Houston(config-if)#`**`frame-relay map ip 172.16.2.2 50`**	Maps the remote IP address to local DLCI 50.
`Houston(config-if)#`**`frame-relay map ip 172.16.2.3 51`**	Maps the remote IP address to local DLCI 51.

Houston(config-if)#**frame-relay map ip 172.16.2.4 52**	Maps the remote IP address to local DLCI 52.
Houston(config-if)#**no shutdown**	Enables the interface.
Houston(config-if)#**exit**	Returns to global configuration mode.
Houston(config)#**router ospf 1**	Starts OSPF process 1.
Houston(config-router)#**network 172.16.0.0 0.0.255.255 area 0**	Any interface with an IP address of 172.16.*x*.*x* will be placed into area 0.
Houston(config-router)#**neighbor 172.16.2.2**	Identifies neighbor (Austin) to Houston.
Houston(config-router)#**neighbor 172.16.2.3**	Identifies neighbor (Galveston) to Houston.
Houston(config-router)#**neighbor 172.16.2.4**	Identifies neighbor (Laredo) to Houston.
Houston(config-router)#**exit**	Returns to global configuration mode
Houston(config)#**exit**	Returns to privileged mode.
Houston#**copy running-config startup-config**	Saves the configuration to NVRAM.

Austin Router

Router>**enable**	Moves to privileged mode.
Router#**configure terminal**	Moves to global configuration mode.
Router(config)#**hostname Austin**	Sets the router host name.
Austin(config)#**interface serial 0/0**	Enters interface configuration mode.
Austin(config-if)#**encapsulation frame-relay**	Enables Frame Relay encapsulation.
Austin(config-if)#**ip address 172.16.2.2 255.255.255.0**	Assigns an IP address and netmask.
Austin(config-if)#**frame-relay map ip 172.16.2.1 150**	Maps the remote IP address to local DLCI 150.
Austin(config-if)#**frame-relay map ip 172.16.2.3 150**	Maps the remote IP address to local DLCI 150.

Austin(config-if)#frame-relay map ip 172.16.2.4 150	Maps the remote IP address to local DLCI 150.
Austin(config-if)#no shutdown	Enables the interface.
Austin(config-if)#exit	Returns to global configuration mode.
Austin(config)#router ospf 1	Starts OSPF process 1.
Austin(config-router)#network 172.16.0.0 0.0.255.255 area 0	Any interface with an IP address of 172.16.x.x will be placed into area 0.
Austin(config-router)#neighbor 172.16.2.1 priority 10	Identifies neighbor (Houston) to Austin and assigns a priority of 10 to Houston for DR/BDR election.
Austin(config-router)#exit	Returns to global configuration mode.
Austin(config)#exit	Returns to privileged mode.
Austin#copy running-config startup-config	Saves the configuration to NVRAM.

Galveston Router

Router>enable	Moves to privileged mode.
Router#configure terminal	Moves to global configuration mode.
Router(config)#hostname Galveston	Sets the router host name.
Galveston(config)#interface serial 0/0	Enters interface configuration mode.
Galveston(config-if)#encapsulation frame-relay	Enables Frame Relay encapsulation.
Galveston(config-if)#ip address 172.16.2.3 255.255.255.0	Assigns an IP address and netmask.
Galveston(config-if)#frame-relay map ip 172.16.2.1 151	Maps the remote IP address to local DLCI 151.
Galveston(config-if)#frame-relay map ip 172.16.2.2 151	Maps the remote IP address to local DLCI 151.
Galveston(config-if)#frame-relay map ip 172.16.2.4 151	Maps the remote IP address to local DLCI 151.
Galveston(config-if)#no shutdown	Enables the interface.
Galveston(config-if)#exit	Returns to global configuration mode.

Galveston(config)#**router ospf 1**	Starts OSPF process 1.
Galveston(config-router)#**network 172.16.0.0 0.0.255.255 area 0**	Any interface with an IP address of 172.16.x.x will be placed into area 0.
Galveston(config-router)#**neighbor 172.16.2.1 priority 10**	Identifies neighbor (Houston) to Galveston and assigns a priority of 10 to Houston for DR/BDR election.
Galveston(config-router)#**exit**	Returns to global configuration mode.
Galveston(config)#**exit**	Returns to privileged mode.
Galveston#**copy running-config startup-config**	Saves the configuration to NVRAM.

Laredo Router

Router>**enable**	Moves to privileged mode.
Router#**configure terminal**	Moves to global configuration mode.
Router(config)#**hostname Laredo**	Sets the router host name.
Laredo(config)#**interface serial 0/0**	Enters interface configuration mode.
Laredo(config-if)#**encapsulation frame-relay**	Enables Frame Relay encapsulation.
Laredo(config-if)#**ip address 172.16.2.4 255.255.255.0**	Assigns an IP address and netmask.
Laredo(config-if)#**frame-relay map ip 172.16.2.1 152**	Maps the remote IP address to local DLCI 152.
Laredo(config-if)#**frame-relay map ip 172.16.2.2 152**	Maps the remote IP address to local DLCI 152.
Laredo(config-if)#**frame-relay map ip 172.16.2.3 152**	Maps the remote IP address to local DLCI 152.
Laredo(config-if)#**no shutdown**	Enables the interface.
Laredo(config-if)#**exit**	Returns to global configuration mode.
Laredo(config)#**router ospf 1**	Starts OSPF process 1.
Laredo(config-router)#**network 172.16.0.0 0.0.255.255 area 0**	Any interface with an IP address of 172.16.x.x will be placed into area 0.

Laredo(config-router)#**neighbor 172.16.2.1 priority 10**	Identifies neighbor (Houston) to Laredo and assigns a priority of 10 to Houston for DR/BDR election.
Laredo(config-router)#**exit**	Returns to global configuration mode.
Laredo(config)#**exit**	Returns to privileged mode.
Laredo#**copy running-config startup-config**	Saves the configuration to NVRAM.

Configuration Example: OSPF and Broadcast Networks

Figure 3-5 shows the network topology for the configuration that follows, which demonstrates how to configure OSPF on a broadcast network using the commands covered in this chapter.

Figure 3-5   Network Topology for OSPF Configuration on a Broadcast Network

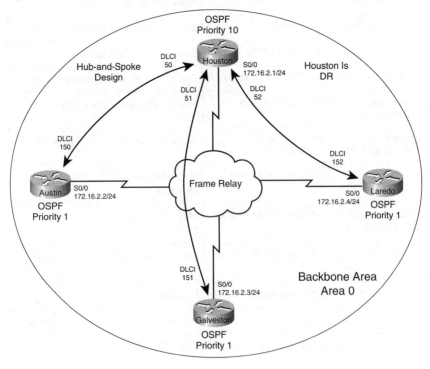

Houston Router

Router>**enable**	Moves to privileged mode.
Router#**configure terminal**	Moves to global configuration mode.
Router(config)#**hostname Houston**	Sets the router host name.
Houston(config)#**interface serial 0/0**	Enters interface configuration mode.
Houston(config-if)#**encapsulation frame-relay**	Enables Frame Relay encapsulation.
Houston(config-if)#**ip address 172.16.2.1 255.255.255.0**	Assigns an IP address and netmask.
Houston(config-if)#**ip ospf network broadcast**	Changes the network type from the default NBMA to broadcast.
Houston(config-if)#**ip ospf priority 10**	Sets the priority to 10 for the DR/BDR election process.
Houston(config-if)#**frame-relay map ip 172.16.2.2 50 broadcast**	Maps the remote IP address to local DLCI 50. Broadcast and multicasts will now be forwarded.
Houston(config-if)#**frame-relay map ip 172.16.2.3 51 broadcast**	Maps the remote IP address to local DLCI 51. Broadcast and multicasts will now be forwarded.
Houston(config-if)#**frame-relay map ip 172.16.2.4 52 broadcast**	Maps the remote IP address to local DLCI 52. Broadcast and multicasts will now be forwarded.
Houston(config-if)#**no shut**	Enables the interface.
Houston(config-if)#**exit**	Returns to global configuration mode.
Houston(config)#**router ospf 1**	Starts OSPF process 1.
Houston(config-router)#**network 172.16.0.0 0.0.255.255 area 0**	Any interface with an IP address of 172.16.*x.x* will be placed into area 0.
Houston(config-router)#**exit**	Returns to global configuration mode.
Houston(config)#**exit**	Returns to privileged mode.
Houston#**copy running-config startup-config**	Saves the configuration to NVRAM.

Austin Router

`Router>`**`enable`**	Moves to privileged mode.
`Router#`**`configure terminal`**	Moves to global configuration mode.
`Router(config)#`**`hostname Austin`**	Sets the router host name.
`Austin(config)#`**`interface serial 0/0`**	Enters interface configuration mode.
`Austin(config-if)#`**`encapsulation frame-relay`**	Enables Frame Relay encapsulation.
`Austin(config-if)#`**`ip address 172.16.2.2 255.255.255.0`**	Assigns an IP address and netmask.
`Austin(config-if)#`**`ip ospf network broadcast`**	Changes the network type from the default NBMA to broadcast.
`Austin(config-if)#`**`ip ospf priority 0`**	Sets the priority to 0 for the DR/BDR election process. Austin will not participate in the election process.
`Austin(config-if)#`**`frame-relay map ip 172.16.2.1 150 broadcast`**	Maps the remote IP address to local DLCI 150. Broadcast and multicasts will now be forwarded.
`Austin(config-if)#`**`frame-relay map ip 172.16.2.3 150 broadcast`**	Maps the remote IP address to local DLCI 150. Broadcast and multicasts will now be forwarded.
`Austin(config-if)#`**`frame-relay map ip 172.16.2.4 150 broadcast`**	Maps the remote IP address to local DLCI 150. Broadcast and multicasts will now be forwarded.
`Austin(config-if)#`**`no shutdown`**	Enables the interface.
`Austin(config-if)#`**`exit`**	Returns to global configuration mode.
`Austin(config)#`**`router ospf 1`**	Starts OSPF process 1.
`Austin(config-router)#`**`network 172.16.0.0 0.0.255.255 area 0`**	Any interface with an IP address of 172.16.$x.x$ will be placed into area 0.
`Austin(config-router)#`**`exit`**	Returns to global configuration mode.
`Austin(config)#`**`exit`**	Returns to privileged mode.
`Austin#`**`copy running-config startup-config`**	Saves the configuration to NVRAM.

Galveston Router

`Router>`**`enable`**	Moves to privileged mode.
`Router#`**`configure terminal`**	Moves to global configuration mode.
`Router(config)#`**`hostname Galveston`**	Sets the router host name.
`Galveston(config)#`**`interface serial 0/0`**	Enters interface configuration mode.
`Galveston(config-if)#`**`encapsulation frame-relay`**	Enables Frame Relay encapsulation.
`Galveston(config-if)#`**`ip address 172.16.2.3 255.255.255.0`**	Assigns an IP address and netmask.
`Galveston(config-if)#`**`ip ospf network broadcast`**	Changes the network type from the default NBMA to broadcast.
`Galveston(config-if)#`**`ip ospf priority 0`**	Sets the priority to 0 for the DR/BDR election process. Galveston will not participate in the election process.
`Galveston(config-if)#`**`frame-relay map ip 172.16.2.1 151 broadcast`**	Maps the remote IP address to local DLCI 151. Broadcast and multicasts will now be forwarded.
`Galveston(config-if)#`**`frame-relay map ip 172.16.2.2 151 broadcast`**	Maps the remote IP address to local DLCI 151. Broadcast and multicasts will now be forwarded.
`Galveston(config-if)#`**`frame-relay map ip 172.16.2.4 151 broadcast`**	Maps the remote IP address to local DLCI 151. Broadcast and multicasts will now be forwarded.
`Galveston(config-if)#`**`no shutdown`**	Enables the interface.
`Galveston(config-if)#`**`exit`**	Returns to global configuration mode.
`Galveston(config)#`**`router ospf 1`**	Starts OSPF process 1.
`Galveston(config-router)#`**`network 172.16.0.0 0.0.255.255 area 0`**	Any interface with an IP address of 172.16.*x.x* will be placed into area 0.
`Galveston(config-router)#`**`exit`**	Returns to global configuration mode.
`Galveston(config)#`**`exit`**	Returns to privileged mode.
`Galveston#`**`copy running-config startup-config`**	Saves the configuration to NVRAM.

Laredo Router

`Router>`**`enable`**	Moves to privileged mode.
`Router#`**`configure terminal`**	Moves to global configuration mode.
`Router(config)#`**`hostname Laredo`**	Sets the router host name.
`Laredo(config)#`**`interface serial 0/0`**	Enters interface configuration mode.
`Laredo(config-if)#`**`encapsulation frame-relay`**	Enables Frame Relay encapsulation.
`Laredo(config-if)#`**`ip address 172.16.2.4 255.255.255.0`**	Assigns an IP address and netmask.
`Laredo(config-if)#`**`ip ospf network broadcast`**	Changes the network type from the default NBMA to broadcast.
`Laredo(config-if)#`**`ip ospf priority 0`**	Sets the priority to 0 for the DR/BDR election process. Laredo will not participate in the election process.
`Laredo(config-if)#`**`frame-relay map ip 172.16.2.1 152 broadcast`**	Maps the remote IP address to local DLCI 152. Broadcast and multicasts will now be forwarded.
`Laredo(config-if)#`**`frame-relay map ip 172.16.2.2 152 broadcast`**	Maps the remote IP address to local DLCI 152. Broadcast and multicasts will now be forwarded.
`Laredo(config-if)#`**`frame-relay map ip 172.16.2.3 152 broadcast`**	Maps the remote IP address to local DLCI 152. Broadcast and multicasts will now be forwarded.
`Laredo(config-if)#`**`no shutdown`**	Enables the interface.
`Laredo(config-if)#`**`exit`**	Returns to global configuration mode.
`Laredo(config)#`**`router ospf 1`**	Starts OSPF process 1.
`Laredo(config-router)#`**`network 172.16.0.0 0.0.255.255 area 0`**	Any interface with an IP address of 172.16.x.x will be placed into area 0.
`Laredo(config-router)#`**`exit`**	Returns to global configuration mode.
`Laredo(config)#`**`exit`**	Returns to privileged mode.
`Laredo#`**`copy running-config startup-config`**	Saves the configuration to NVRAM.

Configuration Example: OSPF and Point-to-Multipoint Networks

Figure 3-6 shows the network topology for the configuration that follows, which demonstrates how to configure OSPF on a point-to-multipoint network using the commands covered in this chapter.

Figure 3-6   Network Topology for OSPF Configuration on a Point-to-Multipoint Network

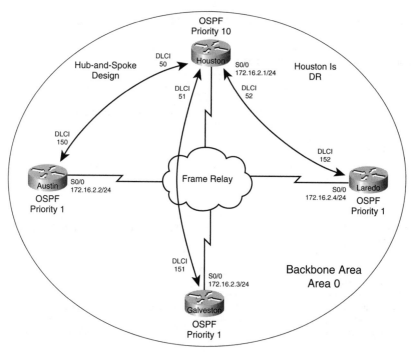

Houston Router

`Router>`**`enable`**	Moves to privileged mode.
`Router#`**`configure terminal`**	Moves to privileged mode.
`Router(config)#`**`hostname Houston`**	Sets the router host name.
`Houston(config)#`**`interface serial 0/0`**	Enters interface configuration mode.
`Houston(config-if)#`**`encapsulation frame-relay`**	Enables Frame Relay encapsulation.
`Houston(config-if)#`**`ip address 172.16.2.1 255.255.255.0`**	Assigns an IP address and netmask.

Houston(config-if)#**ip ospf network point-to-multipoint**	Changes the network type from the default NBMA to point to multipoint.
Houston(config-if)#**frame-relay map ip 172.16.2.2 50**	Maps the remote IP address to local DLCI 50.
Houston(config-if)#**frame-relay map ip 172.16.2.3 51**	Maps the remote IP address to local DLCI 51.
Houston(config-if)#**frame-relay map ip 172.16.2.4 52**	Maps the remote IP address to local DLCI 52.
Houston(config-if)#**no shutdown**	Enables the interface.
Houston(config-if)#**exit**	Returns to global configuration mode.
Houston(config)#**router ospf 1**	Enables OSPF process 1.
Houston(config-router)#**network 172.16.0.0 0.0.255.255 area 0**	Any interface with an IP address of 172.16.*x.x* will be placed into area 0.
Houston(config-router)#**exit**	Returns to global configuration mode.
Houston(config)#**exit**	Returns to privileged mode.
Houston#**copy running-config startup-config**	Saves the configuration to NVRAM.

Austin Router

Router>**enable**	Moves to privileged mode.
Router#**configure terminal**	Moves to global configuration mode.
Router(config)#**hostname Austin**	Sets the router host name.
Austin(config)#**interface serial 0/0**	Enters serial interface mode.
Austin(config-if)#**encapsulation frame-relay**	Enables Frame Relay encapsulation.
Austin(config-if)#**ip address 172.16.2.2 255.255.255.0**	Assigns an IP address and netmask.
Austin(config-if)#**ip ospf network point-to-multipoint**	Changes the network type from the default NBMA to point to multipoint.
Austin(config-if)#**frame-relay map ip 172.16.2.1 150**	Maps the remote IP address to local DLCI 150.
Austin(config-if)#**frame-relay map ip 172.16.2.3 150**	Maps the remote IP address to local DLCI 150.

`Austin(config-if)#frame-relay map ip` `172.16.2.4 150`	Maps the remote IP address to local DLCI 150.
`Austin(config-if)#no shutdown`	Enables the interface.
`Austin(config-if)#exit`	Returns to global configuration mode.
`Austin(config)#router ospf 1`	Starts OSPF process 1.
`Austin(config-router)#network` `172.16.0.0 0.0.255.255 area 0`	Any interface with an IP address of 172.16.*x.x* will be placed into area 0.
`Austin(config-router)#exit`	Returns to global configuration mode.
`Austin(config)#exit`	Returns to privileged mode.
`Austin#copy running-config startup-` `config`	Saves the configuration to NVRAM.

Galveston Router

`Router>enable`	Moves to privileged mode.
`Router#configure terminal`	Moves to global configuration mode.
`Router(config)#hostname Galveston`	Sets the router host name.
`Galveston(config)#interface serial 0/` `0`	Enters interface configuration mode.
`Galveston(config-if)#encapsulation` `frame-relay`	Enables Frame Relay encapsulation.
`Galveston(config-if)#ip address` `172.16.2.3 255.255.255.0`	Assigns an IP address and netmask.
`Galveston(config-if)#ip ospf network` `point-to-multipoint`	Changes the network type from the default NBMA to point to multipoint.
`Galveston(config-if)#frame-relay map` `ip 172.16.2.1 151`	Maps the remote IP address to local DLCI 151.
`Galveston(config-if)#frame-relay map` `ip 172.16.2.2 151`	Maps the remote IP address to local DLCI 151.
`Galveston(config-if)#frame-relay map` `ip 172.16.2.4 151`	Maps the remote IP address to local DLCI 151.
`Galveston(config-if)#no shutdown`	Enables the interface.
`Galveston(config-if)#exit`	Returns to global configuration mode.

Galveston(config)#**router ospf 1**	Starts OSPF process 1.
Galveston(config-router)#**network 172.16.0.0 0.0.255.255 area 0**	Any interface with an IP address of 172.16.x.x will be placed into area 0.
Galveston(config-router)#**exit**	Returns to global configuration mode.
Galveston(config)#**exit**	Returns to privileged mode.
Galveston#**copy running-config startup-config**	Saves the configuration to NVRAM.

Laredo Router

Router>**enable**	Moves to privileged mode.
Router#**configure terminal**	Moves to global configuration mode.
Router(config)#**hostname Laredo**	Sets the router host name.
Laredo(config)#**interface serial 0/0**	Enters interface configuration mode.
Laredo(config-if)#**encapsulation frame-relay**	Enables Frame Relay encapsulation.
Laredo(config-if)#**ip address 172.16.2.4 255.255.255.0**	Assigns an IP address and netmask.
Laredo(config-if)#**ip ospf network point-to-multipoint**	Changes the network type from the default NBMA to point to multipoint.
Laredo(config-if)#**frame-relay map ip 172.16.2.1 152**	Maps the remote IP address to local DLCI 152.
Laredo(config-if)#**frame-relay map ip 172.16.2.2 152**	Maps the remote IP address to local DLCI 152.
Laredo(config-if)#**frame-relay map ip 172.16.2.3 152**	Maps the remote IP address to local DLCI 152.
Laredo(config-if)#**no shut**	Enables the interface.
Laredo(config-if)#**exit**	Returns to global configuration mode.
Laredo(config)#**router ospf 1**	Starts OSPF process 1.
Laredo(config-router)#**network 172.16.0.0 0.0.255.255 area 0**	Any interface with an IP address of 172.16.x.x will be placed into area 0.
Laredo(config-router)#**exit**	Returns to global configuration mode.

Laredo(config)#exit	Returns to privileged mode.
Laredo#copy running-config startup-config	Saves the configuration to NVRAM.

Configuration Example: OSPF and Point-to-Point Networks Using Subinterfaces

Figure 3-7 shows the network topology for the configuration that follows, which demonstrates how to configure OSPF on a point-to-point network using subinterfaces, using the commands covered in this chapter.

Figure 3-7   Network Topology for OSPF Configuration on a Point-to-Point Network Using Subinterfaces

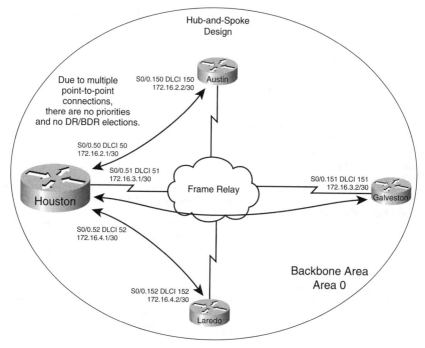

Houston Router

Router>enable	Moves to privileged mode.
Router#configure terminal	Moves to global configuration mode.

`Router(config)#hostname Houston`	Sets the router host name.
`Houston(config)#interface serial 0/0`	Enters interface configuration mode.
`Houston(config-if)#encapsulation frame-relay`	Enables Frame Relay encapsulation.
`Houston(config-if)#no shutdown`	Enables the interface.
`Houston(config-if)#interface serial 0/0.50 point-to-point`	Creates a subinterface.
`Houston(config-subif)#description Link to Austin`	Creates a locally significant description of the interface.
`Houston(config-subif)#ip address 172.16.2.1 255.255.255.252`	Assigns an IP address and netmask.
`Houston(config-subif)#frame-relay interface-dlci 50`	Assigns a DLCI to the subinterface.
`Houston(config-subif)#exit`	Returns to interface configuration mode.
`Houston(config-if)#interface serial 0/0.51 point-to-point`	Creates a subinterface.
`Houston(config-subif)#description Link to Galveston`	Creates a locally significant description of the interface.
`Houston(config-subif)#ip address 172.16.3.1 255.255.255.252`	Assigns an IP address and netmask.
`Houston(config-subif)#frame-relay interface-dlci 51`	Assigns a DLCI to the subinterface.
`Houston(config-subif)#exit`	Returns to interface configuration mode.
`Houston(config-if)#interface serial 0/0.52 point-to-point`	Creates a subinterface.
`Houston(config-subif)#description Link to Laredo`	Creates a locally significant description of the interface.
`Houston(config-subif)#ip address 172.16.4.1 255.255.255.252`	Assigns an IP address and netmask.
`Houston(config-subif)#frame-relay interface-dlci 52`	Assigns a DLCI to the subinterface.
`Houston(config-subif)#exit`	Returns to interface configuration mode.

`Houston(config-if)#exit`	Returns to global configuration mode.
`Houston(config)#router ospf 1`	Starts OSPF process 1.
`Houston(config-router)#network 172.16.0.0 0.0.255.255 area 0`	Any interface with an IP address of 172.16.*x.x* will be placed into area 0.
`Houston(config-router)#exit`	Returns to global configuration mode.
`Houston(config)#exit`	Returns to privileged mode.
`Houston#copy running-config startup-config`	Saves the configuration to NVRAM.

Austin Router

`Router>enable`	Moves to privileged mode.
`Router#configure terminal`	Moves to global configuration mode.
`Router(config)#hostname Austin`	Sets the router host name.
`Austin(config)#interface serial 0/0`	Enters interface configuration mode.
`Austin(config-if)#encapsulation frame-relay`	Enables Frame Relay encapsulation.
`Austin(config-if)#no shutdown`	Enables the interface.
`Austin(config-if)#interface serial 0/0.150 point-to-point`	Creates a subinterface.
`Austin(config-subif)#description Link to Houston`	Creates a locally significant description of the interface.
`Austin(config-subif)#ip address 172.16.2.2 255.255.255.252`	Assigns an IP address and netmask.
`Austin(config-subif)#frame-relay interface-dlci 150`	Assigns a DLCI to the subinterface.
`Austin(config-subif)#exit`	Returns to interface configuration mode.
`Austin(config-if)#exit`	Returns to global configuration mode.
`Austin(config)#router ospf 1`	Starts OSPF process 1.

Austin(config-router)#**network 172.16.0.0 0.0.255.255 area 0**	Any interface with an IP address of 172.16.*x.x* will be placed into area 0.
Austin(config-router)#**exit**	Returns to global configuration mode.
Austin(config)#**exit**	Returns to privileged mode.
Austin#**copy running-config startup-config**	Saves the configuration to NVRAM.

Galveston Router

Router>**enable**	Moves to privileged mode.
Router#**configure terminal**	Moves to global configuration mode.
Router(config)#**hostname Galveston**	Sets the router host name.
Galveston(config)#**interface serial 0/0**	Enters interface configuration mode.
Galveston(config-if)#**encapsulation frame-relay**	Enables Frame Relay encapsulation.
Galveston(config-if)#**no shutdown**	Enables the interface.
Galveston(config-if)#**interface serial 0/0.151 point-to-point**	Creates a subinterface.
Galveston(config-subif)#**description Link to Houston**	Creates a locally significant description of the interface.
Galveston(config-subif)#**ip address 172.16.3.2 255.255.255.252**	Assigns an IP address and netmask.
Galveston(config-subif)#**frame-relay interface-dlci 151**	Assigns a DLCI to the subinterface.
Galveston(config-subif)#**exit**	Returns to interface configuration mode.
Galveston(config-if)#**exit**	Returns to global configuration mode.
Galveston(config)#**router ospf 1**	Starts OSPF process 1.
Galveston(config-router)#**network 172.16.0.0 0.0.255.255 area 0**	Any interface with an IP address of 172.16.*x.x* will be placed into area 0.
Galveston(config-router)#**exit**	Returns to global configuration mode.
Galveston(config)#**exit**	Returns to privileged mode.
Galveston#**copy running-config startup-config**	Saves the configuration to NVRAM.

Laredo Router

`Router>`**`enable`**	Moves to privileged mode.
`Router#`**`configure terminal`**	Moves to global configuration mode.
`Router(config)#`**`hostname Laredo`**	Sets the router host name.
`Laredo(config)#`**`interface serial 0/0`**	Enters interface configuration mode.
`Laredo(config-if)#`**`encapsulation frame-relay`**	Enables Frame Relay encapsulation.
`Laredo(config-if)#`**`no shutdown`**	Enables the interface.
`Laredo(config-if)#`**`interface serial 0/0.152 point-to-point`**	Creates a subinterface.
`Laredo(config-subif)#`**`description Link to Houston`**	Creates a locally significant description of the interface.
`Laredo(config-subif)#`**`ip address 172.16.4.2 255.255.255.252`**	Assigns an IP address and netmask.
`Laredo(config-subif)#`**`frame-relay interface-dlci 152`**	Assigns a DLCI to sthe ubinterface.
`Laredo(config-subif)#`**`exit`**	Returns to interface configuration mode.
`Laredo(config-if)#`**`exit`**	Returns to global configuration mode.
`Laredo(config)#`**`router ospf 1`**	Starts OSPF process 1.
`Laredo(config-router)#`**`network 172.16.0.0 0.0.255.255 area 0`**	Any interface with an IP address of 172.16.*x*.*x* will be placed into area 0.
`Laredo(config-router)#`**`exit`**	Returns to global configuration mode.
`Laredo(config)#`**`exit`**	Returns to privileged mode.
`Laredo#`**`copy running-config startup-config`**	Saves the configuration to NVRAM.

CHAPTER 4

Integrated IS-IS

This chapter provides information and commands concerning the following
Intermediate System-to-Intermediate System (IS-IS) topics:

- ISO Network Entity Title (NET)
- Rules for creating a NET
- Examples of NETs: Cisco implementation
- Basic IS-IS configuration
- Neighbors and timers
- Election of the designated IS (DIS)
- Rules for IS-IS adjacencies
- Routing metrics
- Wide metrics
- Manual summarization
- Injecting default routes
- Defining router types
- Verifying integrated IS-IS routing
- Configuration example: Multi-area IS-IS

ISO Network Entity Title (NET)

Figure 4-1 shows three of the different formats that an ISO NET can take:

> (a) An 8-octet area IS/system ID format
> (b) An OSI NSAP format
> (c) A GOSIP NSAP format

Figure 4-1   *Formats for ISO NET*

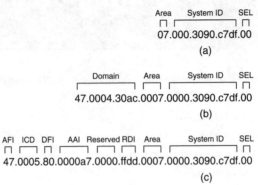

Rules for Creating a NET

- The NET must begin with a single octet.
- Addresses starting with 49 (AF I= 49) are considered private IP address, analogous to RFC 1918.
  - Routed by IS-IS
  - Should not be advertised to other Connectionless Network Service (CLNS) networks (outside this IS-IS domain)
- Additional 2 bytes added for the area ID.
- All routers in the same area must have the same area address.
- The system ID must be the same number of octets throughout the domain.
- Cisco has implemented a fixed length of 6 octets for the system ID of a NET.
- It is customary to use the MAC address of the router, or an IP address of a loopback interface (192.168.111.3 = 192.168.111.003 = 1921.6811.1003).
- The practice of using a modified loopback IP address as the system ID may now be considered outdated because of the dynamic host name feature. This feature uses a new Type Length Value (TLV 137) to map the router's host name to the system ID.
- Each device must have a unique system ID within the area.
- The NET must end with a single octet—the network service access point (NSAP) selector byte (NSEL), usually set to 0x00.
  - When the NSEL is set to 0, it identifies the device itself.
  - The NSEL is like a TCP port number: It indicates the transport layer.

Examples of NETs: Cisco Implementation

Example 1: NSAP **47.0001**.*aaaa.bbbb.cccc*.**00**

Area ID is **47.0001**
System ID is *aaaa.bbbb.cccc*
NSAP selector byte is **00**

Example 2: NSAP **39.0f01.0002**.*0000.0c00.1111*.**00**

Area ID is **39.0f01.0002**
System ID is *0000.0c00.1111*
NSAP selector byte is **00**

Basic IS-IS Configuration

NOTE: IS-IS is the only IP routing protocol that must be enabled both as a process and on individual interfaces.

`Router(config)#`**`router isis`**	Enables the IS-IS routing process.
`Router(config-router)#`**`network`** **`49.0001.1111.1111.1111.00`**	Configures the NET.
`Router(config-router)#`**`exit`**	Returns to global configuration mode.
`Router(config)#`**`interface`** **`fastethernet 0/0`**	Enters interface configuration mode.
`Router(config-if)#`**`ip address`** **`172.16.1.1 255.255.255.0`**	Assigns the IP address and netmask.
`Router(config-if)#`**`ip router isis`**	Enables IS-IS routing on this interface. A "null" tag (area designator) is used for the routing process if no area tag is given.
	TIP: You cannot issue an **ip router isis** command on an interface until an IP address has been assigned to that interface.
	NOTE: The **ip router isis** command must be added to all interfaces whose networks are to be advertised by IS-IS. This includes transit interfaces (interfaces connected to IS-IS neighbors) and interfaces connected to stub networks (interfaces not connected to IS-IS networks).

`Router(config-if)#no shutdown`	Activates the interface.
`Router(config-if)#exit`	Returns to global configuration mode.

Neighbors and Timers

`Router(config)#interface fastethernet 0/0`	Enters interface configuration mode.
`Router(config-if)#isis hello-interval 20`	Changes the interval to 20 seconds between exchanges of Hello protocol data units (PDU). The default is 10 seconds.
	NOTE: A faster hello interval facilitates faster convergence but increases bandwidth and CPU use. It might also add to instability in the network. A slower hello interval saves bandwidth and CPU use.
`Router(config-if)#isis hello-multiplier 4`	Changes the length of the hold-time multiplier. By default, an IS-IS router waits 3 times the hello interval until it considers a neighbor dead.
	TIP: The **isis hello-interval** and the **isis hello-multiplier** commands are changed on a per-interface basis. Timers can vary on different interfaces.
	NOTE: It makes more sense to tune the hello interval and hello multiplier on point-to-point interfaces than on LAN interfaces.
	NOTE: Hello intervals and hold times do *not* have to match between IS-IS neighbors for an adjacency to form.

Election of the Designated IS (DIS)

`Router(config)#interface fastethernet 0/0`	Enters interface configuration mode.
`Router(config-if)#isis priority 100`	Changes the priority to 100 for the DIS election process.
	NOTE: DIS priority is a number that ranges from 0 to 127. The Cisco default is 64. The highest priority wins the DIS election. If all priorities are the same, the numerically highest MAC address wins the election. There is no way to make a router ineligible from being the DIS—there is no IS-IS equivalent to the **OSPF priority 0** option.
	NOTE: There is *no* backup DIS.

Rules for IS-IS Adjacencies

- L1 routers form L1 adjacencies with L1 and L1-L2 routers in their area.
- L2 routers form L2 adjacencies with L2 and L1-L2 routers in their area or another area.
- L1/L2 routers form L1 and L2 adjacencies with each other in their area or another area.
- An L1 router does *not* form an adjacency with an L2 router, regardless of area.
- The system ID must be unique to each router.
- Hello intervals and hold times do *not* have to match.

Routing Metrics

`Router(config)#interface serial 0/0`	Enters interface configuration mode.
`Router(config-if)#isis metric 50`	Changes the metric to 50. The range is from 0 to 63.
	NOTE: The default metric for IS-IS is 10, regardless of interface type. This makes hop count the IS-IS routing metric, if all interfaces are left at the default metric.

	NOTE: The total cost of any route is a sum of the individual metrics of the outgoing interfaces.
	NOTE: The maximum metric value is 1023.

Wide Metrics

Router(config)#**router isis**	Enables the IS-IS routing process.
Router(config-router)#**metric-style wide**	Enables the wide metric.
	NOTE: To support better metric granularity, Cisco IOS Software allows for a wider metric field. This field could be 24 bits wide for the Extended IP Reachability TLV or 32 bits wide for the Extended IP Reachability TLV. These fields are used primarily when working with traffic engineering.

Manual Summarization

Router(config)#**router isis**	Enables the IS-IS routing process.
Router(config-router)#**summary-address 192.168.0.0 255.255.255.240**	Enables manual summarization for the given address and netmask.

Injecting Default Routes

Router(config)#**ip route 0.0.0.0 0.0.0.0 172.16.0.1**	Creates a default route.
Router(config)#**router isis**	Enables the IS-IS routing process.
Router(config-router)#**default-information originate**	Injects the default route into the IS-IS routing domain.

	NOTE: Using the **default-information originate** command will inform a router that it is an interdomain router.
	NOTE: The **default-information originate** command will only be used on an L2 or an L1/L2 router.

Defining Router Types

`Router(config)#router isis`	Enables the IS-IS routing process.
`Router(config-router)#is-type level-1`	The router will perform only Level 1 routing (intra-area or within a single area).
`Router(config-router)#is-type level-1-2`	The router will perform both Level 1 routing (intra-area) and Level 2 routing (inter-area).
`Router(config-router)#is-type level-2-only`	The router will perform only Level 2 routing. This router will not communicate with Level 1 routers in its own area.
	NOTE: The default for an IS-IS router is to perform both Level 1 *and* Level 2 routing.

Verifying Integrated IS-IS Routing

`Router#show clns neighbor`	Displays both ES and IS neighbor information.
`Router#show isis database`	Displays the IS-IS link-state database in summary form.
`Router#show isis database detail`	Displays the IS-IS link-state database. The contents of each link-state packet are also displayed.
`Router#show ip route`	Displays the current state of the routing table.
`Router#show isis topology`	Displays a list of all connected routers in all areas.

Configuration Example: Multi-Area IS-IS

Figure 4-2 shows the network topology for the configuration that follows, which demonstrates how to configure Integrated IS-IS using the commands covered in this chapter.

Figure 4-2   Multi-Area IS-IS

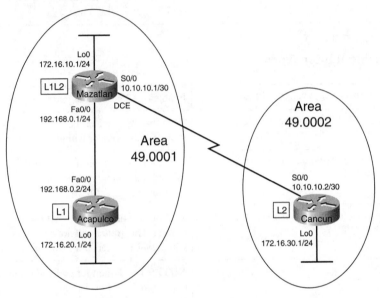

Mazatlan Router

`Router>`**`enable`**	Moves to privileged mode.
`Router#`**`configure terminal`**	Moves to global configuration mode.
`Router(config)#`**`hostname Mazatlan`**	Assigns the host name to the router.
`Mazatlan(config)#`**`interface fastethernet 0/0`**	Enters interface configuration mode.
`Mazatlan(config-if)#`**`ip address 192.168.0.1 255.255.255.0`**	Assigns an IP address and netmask.
`Mazatlan(config-if)#`**`ip router isis`**	Enables IS-IS routing on this interface.

Mazatlan(config-if)#`no shutdown`	Enables the interface.
Mazatlan(config-if)#`int loopback 0`	Moves to interface configuration mode.
Mazatlan(config-if)#`ip address 172.16.10.1 255.255.255.0`	Assigns an IP address and netmask.
Mazatlan(config-if)#`ip router isis`	Enables IS-IS routing on this interface.
Mazatlan(config-if)#`interface serial 0/0`	Moves to interface configuration mode.
Mazatlan(config-if)#`ip address 10.10.10.1 255.255.255.252`	Assigns an IP address and netmask.
Mazatlan(config-if)#`ip router isis`	Enables IS-IS routing on this interface.
Mazatlan(config-if)#`clock rate 56000`	Sets the clock rate.
Mazatlan(config-if)#`no shutdown`	Enables the interface.
Mazatlan(config-if)#`exit`	Returns to global configuration mode.
Mazatlan(config)#`router isis`	Enables the IS-IS routing process.
Mazatlan(config-router)#`net 49.0001.1111.1111.1111.00`	Configures the NET.
Mazatlan(config-router)#`is-type level-1-2`	The router will perform both Level 1 and 2 routing.
Mazatlan(config-router)#`exit`	Returns to global configuration mode.
Mazatlan(config)#`exit`	Returns to privileged mode.
Mazatlan#`copy running-config startup-config`	Saves the configuration to NVRAM.

Acapulco Router

Router>`enable`	Moves to privileged mode.
Router#`configure terminal`	Moves to global configuration mode.
Router(config)#`hostname Acapulco`	Assigns the host name to the router.

Acapulco(config)#**interface fastethernet 0/0**	Enters interface configuration mode.
Acapulco(config-if)#**ip address 192.168.0.2 255.255.255.0**	Assigns an IP address and netmask.
Acapulco(config-if)#**ip router isis**	Enables IS-IS routing on this interface.
Acapulco(config-if)#**no shut**	Enables the interface.
Acapulco(config-if)#**interface loopback 0**	Moves to interface configuration mode.
Acapulco(config-if)#**ip address 172.16.20.1 255.255.255.0**	Assigns an IP address and netmask.
Acapulco(config-if)#**ip router isis**	Enables IS-IS routing on this interface.
Acapulco(config-if)#**exit**	Returns to global configuration mode.
Acapulco(config)#**router isis**	Enables the IS-IS routing process.
Acapulco(config-router)#**net 49.0001.2222.2222.2222.00**	Configures the NET.
Acapulco(config-router)#**is-type level-1**	The router will perform Level 1 routing only.
Acapulco(config-router)#**exit**	Returns to global configuration mode.
Acapulco(config)#**exit**	Returns to privileged mode.
Acapulco#**copy running-config startup-config**	Saves the configuration to NVRAM.

Cancun Router

Router>**enable**	Moves to privileged mode.
Router#**configure terminal**	Moves to global configuration mode.
Router(config)#**hostname Cancun**	Assigns a host name to the router.
Cancun(config)#**interface serial 0/0**	Enters interface configuration mode.
Cancun(config-if)#**ip address 10.10.10.2 255.255.255.252**	Assigns an IP address and netmask.

`Cancun(config-if)#ip router isis`	Enables IS-IS routing on this interface.
`Cancun(config-if)#no shutdown`	Starts the interface.
`Cancun(config-if)#interface loopback 0`	Moves to interface configuration mode.
`Cancun(config-if)#ip address 172.16.30.1 255.255.255.0`	Assigns an IP address and netmask.
`Cancun(config-if)#ip router isis`	Enables IS-IS routing on this interface.
`Cancun(config-if)#exit`	Returns to global configuration mode.
`Cancun(config)#router isis`	Enables the IS-IS routing process.
`Cancun(config-router)#net 49.0002.3333.3333.3333.00`	Configures the NET.
`Cancun(config-router)#is-type level-2-only`	Router will perform Level 2 routing only.
`Cancun(config-router)#exit`	Returns to global configuration mode.
`Cancun(config)#exit`	Returns to privileged mode.
`Cancun#copy running-config startup-config`	Saves the configuration to NVRAM.

CHAPTER 5

Manipulating Routing Updates

This chapter provides information and commands concerning the following manipulating routing updates topics:

- Route redistribution
    - Assigning metrics
    - Redistributing subnets
    - Assigning E1 or E2 routes in OSPF
    - Defining seed metrics
    - Redistributing static routes
    - Assigning metric and router types in IS-IS
    - Redistributing OSPF internal and external routes
    - Verifying route redistribution
- Passive interfaces
- Route filtering using the **distribute-list** command
- Verifying route filters
- Configuration example: Outbound route filters
- Configuration example: Inbound route filters
- "Passive" EIGRP interfaces
- Policy routing using route maps
- Configuration example: Route maps
- Administrative distance (AD)
- Static routes: **permanent** keyword
- Floating static routes
- Static routes and recursive lookups
- DHCP configuration
- Verifying and troubleshooting DHCP configuration
- Configuring a DHCP helper address
- DHCP client on a Cisco IOS Ethernet interface
- Configuration example: DHCP

Route Redistribution

Cisco routers support up to 30 dynamic routing processes. These can be different protocols—such as Open Shortest Path First (OSPF), Enhanced Interior Gateway Protocol (EIGRP), Intermediate System-to-Intermediate System (IS-IS), Routing Information Protocol (RIP), and so on—or the same protocol, but multiple processes of it, such as EIGRP 10 and EIGRP 15. Multiple instances of the same routing protocol are not recommended.

To support multiple routing protocols within the same internetwork efficiently, routing information must be shared among the different protocols. For example, routes learned from an OSPF process might need to be imported into an EIGRP process.

The process of exchanging routing information between routing protocols is called *route redistribution*.

Assigning Metrics

`Router(config)#router rip`	Starts the RIP routing process.
`Router(config-router)#redistribute eigrp 10 metric 3`	Redistributes routes learned from EIGRP autonomous system 10. The **metric** keyword assigns a starting metric of 3 for RIP—in the case of RIP, 3 hops.
`Router(config-router)#default-metric 3`	Assigns a starting metric of 3 for all routes being redistributed into RIP.

NOTE: If both the **metric** keyword in the **redistribute** command and the **default-metric** command are used, the value of the **metric** keyword in the **redistribute** command takes precedence.

TIP: If a value is not specified for the **metric** option, and no value is specified using the **default-metric** command, the default metric value is 0, except for OSPF, where the default cost is 20. Zero is only understood by IS-IS and not by RIP or EIGRP. RIP and EIGRP must have the appropriate metrics assigned to any redistributed routes; otherwise, redistribution will not work.

TIP: In the **redistribution** command, use a value for the **metric** argument that is consistent with the destination protocol.

TIP: The **default-metric** command is useful when routes are being redistributed from more than one source because it eliminates the need for defining the metrics separately for each redistribution.

Redistributing Subnets

`Router(config)#`**`router ospf 1`**	Starts the OSPF routing process.
`Router(config-router)#`**`redistribute eigrp 10 metric 100 subnets`**	Redistributes routes learned from EIGRP autonomous system 10. A metric of 100 is assigned to all routes. Subnets will also be redistributed.
	NOTE: Without the **subnets** command, only the classful address would be redistributed.
`Router(config)#`**`router ospf 1`**	Starts the OSPF routing process.
`Router(config-router)#`**`redistribute connected`**	Redistributes all directly connected networks.
	NOTE: The **connected** keyword refers to routes that are established automatically by virtue of having enabled IP on an interface. For routing protocols such as OSPF and IS-IS, these routes will be redistributed as external to the autonomous system.
`Router(config-router)#`**`redistribute connected metric 50`**	Redistributes all directly connected networks and assigns them a starting metric of 50.
	NOTE: The **redistribute connected** command is *not* affected by the **default-metric** command.

Assigning E1 or E2 Routes in OSPF

`Router(config)#`**`router ospf 1`**	Starts the OSPF routing process.
`Router(config-router)#`**`redistribute eigrp 1 metric-type 1`**	Redistributes routes learned from EIGRP autonomous system 1. Routes will be advertised as E1 routes.
	NOTE: If the **metric-type** argument is not used, routes will be advertised in OSPF as E2 routes. E2 routes have a fixed cost associated with them. The metric will not change as the route is propagated throughout the OSPF area. E1 routes will have internal area costs added to the seed metric.

Defining Seed Metrics

`Router(config)#router eigrp 100`	Starts the EIGRP routing process.
`Router(config-router)#redistribute ospf 1 metric 10000 100 255 1 1500`	Redistributes routes learned from OSPF process 1. The metrics assigned to these routes will be as follows: 10000 = Bandwidth in kbps 100 = Delay in microseconds 255 = Reliability out of 255 1 = Load out of 255 1500 = Maximum transmission unit (MTU) size

NOTE: The values used in this command constitute the *seed metric* for these routes. The seed metric is the initial value of an imported route.

NOTE: RIP and EIGRP must have the appropriate metrics assigned to any redistributed routes; otherwise, redistribution will not work.

TIP: Redistributed routes between EIGRP processes do not need metrics configured. Redistributed routes are tagged as EIGRP external routes and will appear in the routing table with a code of D EX.

Redistributing Static Routes

`Router(config)#router isis`	Starts the IS-IS routing process.
`Router(config-router)#redistribute static`	Redistributes static routes on this router into the IS-IS routing process.

Assigning Metric and Router Types in IS-IS

`Router(config)#router isis`	Starts the IS-IS routing process.
`Router(config-router)#redistribute eigrp 1 metric 0 metric-type internal level-2`	Redistributes routes learned from EIGRP autonomous system 1. An initial metric of 0 is assigned. The routes will be redistributed with internal metrics and as Level 2 routes.

	NOTE: In IS-IS, routes may be redistributed with either internal (default) or external metrics. Routes may also be redistributed as either Level 1 or Level 2 (default) routes. An internal metric value will be lower than 64. An external metric will have a value of between 64 and 128.

Redistributing OSPF Internal and External Routes

Router(config)#**router eigrp 10**	Starts the EIGRP routing process for autonomous system 10.
Router(config-router)#**redistribute ospf 1 match internal external 1 external 2**	Redistributes routes learned from OSPF process ID 1. The keywords **match internal external 1** and **external 2** instruct EIGRP to redistribute internal OSPF routes (and external Type 1 and Type 2 routes).
	NOTE: The default behavior when redistributing OSPF routes is to redistribute all routes—internal, external 1, and external 2. The keywords **match internal external 1** and **external 2** are required only if router behavior is to be modified.

Verifying Route Redistribution

Router#**show ip route**	Displays the current state of the routing table.
Router#**show ip eigrp topology**	Displays the EIGRP topology table.
Router#**show isis database**	Displays the IS-IS link-state database.
Router#**show ip protocols**	Displays parameters and the current state of any active routing process.
Router#**show ip rip database**	Displays summary address entries in the RIP routing database.

Passive Interfaces

`Router(config)#`**`router rip`**	Starts the RIP routing process.
`Router(config-router)#`**`passive-`**`interface s0/0`	Sets the interface as passive—meaning routing updates will not be sent out this interface.
	NOTE: For RIP, the **passive-interface** command will prevent the interface from sending out routing updates but will allow the interface to receive updates.
`Router(config)#`**`router rip`**	Starts the RIP routing process.
`Router(config-router)#`**`passive-`**`interface default`	Sets all interfaces as passive.
	TIP: The **passive-interface default** command is useful for Internet service provider (ISP) and large enterprise networks where a distribution router may have as many as 200 interfaces.
`Router(config-router)#`**`no passive-`**`interface fa0/0`	Activates the Fast Ethernet interface to send and receive updates.
	CAUTION: When the **passive-interface** command is used with EIGRP, inbound and outbound hello packets are prevented from being sent. This will not allow EIGRP neighbors to be created.
	CAUTION: When the **passive-interface** command is used with OSPF, routing information is not sent or received through that interface. This will prevent routers from becoming neighbors on that interface. A better way to control OSPF routing updates is to create a stub area, a totally stubby area, or a not so stubby area (NSSA).
`Router(config)#`**`router isis`**	Starts the IS-IS routing process.
`Router(config-router)#`**`passive-`**`interface loopback 0`	Sets the interface as passive.

NOTE: In IS-IS, a passive interface will only advertise its IP address in its link-state packets (LSP). The interface will not send or receive IS-IS packets.

Route Filtering Using the distribute-list Command

`Router(config)#router eigrp 10`	Starts the EIGRP routing process for autonomous system 10.
`Router(config-router)#distribute-list 1 in`	Creates an incoming global distribute list that refers to access control list (ACL) 1.
`Router(config-router)#distribute-list 2 out`	Creates an outgoing global distribute list that refers to ACL 2.
`Router(config-router)#distribute-list 3 in ethernet 0`	Creates an incoming distribute list for interface Ethernet 0 and refers to ACL 3.
`Router(config-router)#distribute-list 4 out serial 0`	Creates an outgoing distribute list for interface serial 0 and refers to ACL 4.

Verifying Route Filters

`Router#show ip protocols`	Displays the parameters and current state of active routing protocols.

`Routing Protocol is "eigrp 10"`
`  Outgoing update filter list for all interfaces is 2`
`    Serial 0/0 filtered by 4`
`  Incoming update filter list for all interfaces is 1`
`    Ethernet0 filtered by 3`	

NOTE: For each interface and routing process, Cisco IOS Software permits the following:

- One incoming global distribute list
- One outgoing global distribute list
- One incoming interface distribute list
- One outgoing interface distribute list

CAUTION: Route filters have *no* effect on link-state advertisements or the link-state database—a basic requirement of link-state routing protocols is that routers in an area must have identical link-state databases.

NOTE: A route filter can influence the routing table of the router on which the filter is configured but has no effect on the route entries of neighboring routers.

NOTE: OSPF routes *cannot* be filtered from entering the OSPF database. The **distribute-list in** command filters routes only from entering the routing table, but it doesn't prevent LSPs from being propagated.

The command **distribute-list out** works only on the routes being redistributed by the Autonomous System Boundary Routers (ASBR) into OSPF. It can be applied to external Type 2 and external Type 1 routes but *not* to intra-area and interarea routes.

Configuration Example: Outbound Route Filters

Figure 5-1 shows the network topology for the configuration that follows, which demonstrates how to configure outbound route filters to control routing updates using the commands covered in this chapter.

Figure 5-1   Network Topology for Outbound Route Filter Configuration

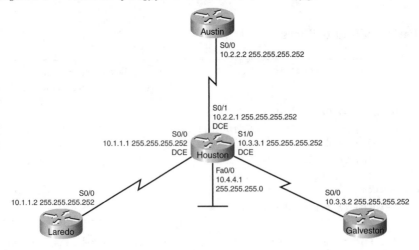

The objective is to prevent subnet 10.1.1.0 from entering Galveston in any EIGRP update from Houston.

Houston Router

Router>`enable`	Moves to privileged mode.
Router#`configure terminal`	Moves to global configuration mode.
Router(config)#`hostname Houston`	Assigns a locally significant host name to the router.
Houston(config)#`interface serial 0/0`	Moves to interface configuration mode.
Houston(config-if)#`ip address 10.1.1.1 255.255.255.252`	Configures an IP address and netmask.
Houston(config-if)#`clock rate 56000`	Sets the clock rate for the interface.
Houston(config-if)#`no shutdown`	Enables the interface.
Houston(config-if)#`interface serial 0/1`	Moves to interface configuration mode.
Houston(config-if)#`ip address 10.2.2.1 255.255.255.252`	Configures an IP address and netmask.
Houston(config-if)#`no shutdown`	Enables the interface.
Houston(config-if)#`interface serial 1/0`	Moves to interface configuration mode.
Houston(config-if)#`ip address 10.3.3.1 255.255.255.252`	Configures an IP address and netmask.
Houston(config-if)#`clock rate 56000`	Sets the clock rate for the interface.
Houston(config-if)#`no shutdown`	Enables the interface.
Houston(config-if)#`interface fastethernet 0/0`	Moves to interface configuration mode.
Houston(config-if)#`ip address 10.4.4.1 255.255.255.0`	Configures an IP address and netmask.
Houston(config-if)#`no shutdown`	Enables the interface.
Houston(config-if)#`exit`	Returns to global configuration mode.

`Houston(config)#router eigrp 10`	Enables the EIGRP routing process for autonomous system 10.
`Houston(config-router)#network 10.0.0.0`	Advertises network 10.0.0.0.
`Houston(config-router)#distribute-list 2 out`	Creates an outgoing global distribute list that refers to ACL 2.
OR	
`Houston(config-router)#distribute-list 2 out serial 1/0`	Creates an outgoing distribute list for interface serial 1/0 that refers to ACL 2.
`Houston(config-router)#exit`	Returns to global configuration mode.
`Houston(config)#access-list 2 deny 10.1.1.0 0.0.0.255`	Read this line to say "All routing updates with an address of 10.1.1.x will be denied and not sent out, based on the parameters of distribute list 2."
`Houston(config)#access-list 2 permit any`	Read this line to say "All routing updates will be permitted to be sent out, based on the parameters of distribute list 2."

If the first **distribute-list** command is used, the EIGRP entry for 10.1.1.0 will not be sent out *any* interface. If the second **distribute-list** command is used, the EIGRP entry for 10.1.1.0 will not be sent out interface serial 1/0 but will be sent out other interfaces as per the rules of EIGRP updates.

Configuration Example: Inbound Route Filters

Figure 5-2 shows the network topology for the configuration that follows, which shows how to configure inbound route filters to control routing updates using the commands covered in this chapter.

Figure 5-2   Network Topology for Inbound Route Filter Configuration

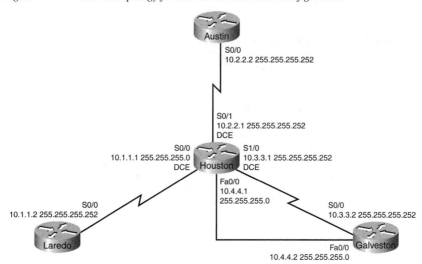

The objective is to prevent subnet 10.1.1.0 from entering Galveston in any EIGRP update from Houston.

Galveston Router

`Router>`**`enable`**	Moves to privileged mode.
`Router#`**`configure terminal`**	Moves to global configuration mode.
`Router(config)#`**`hostname Galveston`**	Sets the router host name.
`Galveston(config)#`**`interface serial 0/0`**	Moves to interface configuration mode.
`Galveston(config-if)#`**`ip address 10.3.3.2 255.255.255.252`**	Assigns an IP address and netmask.
`Galveston(config-if)#`**`interface fasthethernet 0/0`**	Moves to interface configuration mode.
`Galveston(config-if)#`**`ip address 10.4.4.2 255.255.255.0`**	Assigns an IP address and netmask.

`Galveston(config-if)#exit`	Returns to global configuration mode.
`Galveston(config-router)#network 10.0.0.0`	Advertises network 10.0.0.0.
`Galveston(config-router)#distribute-list 1 in`	Creates an incoming global distribute list that refers to ACL 1.
Or	
`Galveston(config-router)#distribute-list 1 in serial 0/0`	Creates an incoming distribute list for interface s0/0 and refers to ACL 1.
`Galveston(config-router)#exit`	Returns to global configuration mode.
`Galveston(config)#access-list 1 deny 10.1.1.0 0.0.0.255`	Read this line to say "All routing updates with an address of 10.1.1.x will be denied and not processed based on the parameters of distribute list 1."
`Galveston(config)#access-list 1 permit any`	Read this line to say "All routing updates will be permitted based on the parameters of distribute list 1."

If the first **distribute-list** command is used, the EIGRP entry for 10.1.1.0 will be filtered out of the routing update from Houston on *all* interfaces. If the second **distribute-list** command is used, the EIGRP entry for 10.1.1.0 will be filtered out from the routing update received on interface s0/0, but the entry will be allowed through interface fa0/0.

"Passive" EIGRP Interfaces

`Router(config)#router eigrp 110`	Starts the EIGRP routing process.
`Router(config-router)#network 10.0.0.0`	Specifies a network to advertise in the EIGRP routing process.
`Router(config-router)#distribute-list 5 out serial 0/0`	Creates an outgoing distribute list for interface serial 0/0 and refers to ACL 5.

`Router(config-router)#exit`	Returns to global configuration mode.
`Router(config)#access-list 5 deny any`	Read this line to say "All routing packets will be denied and not processed based on the parameters of distribute list 5."

NOTE: A passive interface *cannot* send EIGRP hellos, which prevents adjacency relationships with link partners.

An administrator can create a "pseudo" passive EIGRP interface by using a **route filter** that suppresses *all* routes from the EIGRP routing update.

Policy Routing Using Route Maps

`Router(config)#route-map ISP1 permit 20`	Creates a route map named ISP1. This route map will permit traffic based on subsequent criteria. A sequence number of 20 is assigned.
	NOTE: In route maps, the default action is to permit.
	NOTE: The *sequence-number* is used to indicate what position the route map is to have in a list of route maps configured with the same name. If no sequence number is given, the first condition in the route map is automatically numbered as 10.
`Router(config-route-map)#match ip address 1`	Specifies the match criteria (the conditions that should be tested); in this case, match addresses filtered using ACL 1.
`Router(config-route-map)#set interface serial 0/0`	Specifies the set actions (what action is to be performed if the match criteria is met); in this case, forward packets out interface serial 0/0.
`Router(config-route-map)#exit`	Returns to global configuration mode.
`Router(config)#interface fastethernet 0/0`	Moves to interface configuration mode.
`Router(config-if)#ip policy route-map ISP1`	Applies the route map to the appropriate LAN interface.

Configuration Example: Route Maps

Figure 5-3 shows the network topology for the configuration that follows, which demostrates how to configure route maps using the commands covered in this chapter.

Figure 5-3   *Network Topology for Route Map Configuration*

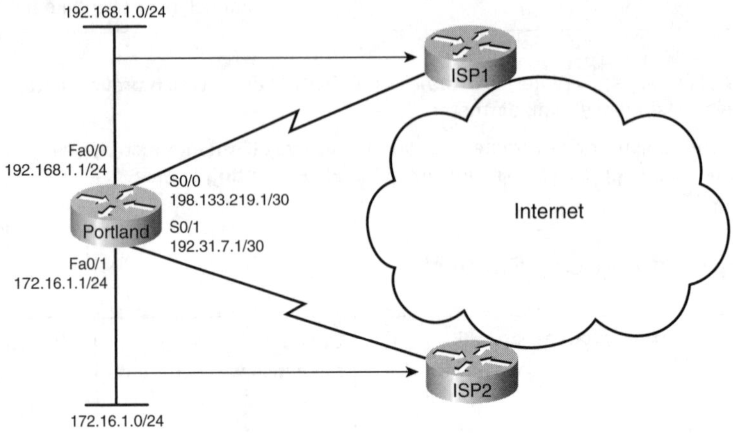

Assume for this example that the policy we want to enforce is this:

- Internet-bound traffic from 192.168.1.0 /24 is to be routed to ISP1.
- Internet-bound traffic from 172.16.1.0 /24 is to be routed to ISP2.
- All other traffic to be routed normally according to their destination addresses.

Portland Router

`Router>`**`enable`**	Moves to privileged mode.
`Router#`**`configure terminal`**	Moves to global configuration mode.
`Router(config)#`**`hostname Portland`**	Sets the host name of this router.
`Portland(config)#`**`access-list 1 permit 192.168.1.0 0.0.0.255`**	Creates ACL 1, which will filter out addresses for our first route map.
`Portland(config)#`**`access-list 2 permit 172.16.1.0 0.0.0.255`**	Creates ACL 2, which will filter out addresses for our second route map.
`Portland(config)#`**`access-list 101 permit ip 192.168.1.0 0.0.0.255 172.16.1.0 0.0.0.255`**	Creates an extended ACL, resulting in a filter based on both source and destination IP address.

Portland(config)#**access-list 102 permit ip 172.16.1.0 0.0.0.255 192.168.1.0 0.0.0.255**	Creates an extended ACL, resulting in a filter based on both source and destination IP address.
Portland(config)#**route-map ISP1 permit 10**	Creates a route map called ISP1. This route map will permit traffic based on subsequent criteria. A sequence number of 10 is assigned.
Portland(config-route-map)#**match ip address 1**	Specifies the match criteria— match addresses filtered from ACL 1.
Portland(config-route-map)#**set interface serial 0/0**	Specifies the set actions (what action is to be performed if the match criteria is met); in this case, forward packets out interface s0/0.
Portland(config-route-map)#**exit**	Returns to global configuration mode.
Portland(config)#**route-map ISP2 permit 10**	Creates a route map called ISP2.
Portland(config-route-map)#**match ip address 2**	Specifies the match criteria— match addresses filtered from ACL 2.
Portland(config-route-map)#**set interface serial 0/1**	Specifies the set actions (what action is to be performed if the match criteria is met); in this case, forward packets out interface s0/1.
Portland(config-route-map)#**exit**	Returns to global configuration mode.
Portland(config)#**route-map 192To172 permit 10**	Creates a route map named 192To172. This route map will permit traffic based on subsequent criteria. A sequence number of 10 is assigned.
Portland(config-route-map)#**match ip address 101**	Specifies the match criteria— match addresses filtered from ACL 101.
Portland(config-route-map)#**set interface fastethernet 0/1**	Specifies the set actions—forward packets out interface fastethernet 0/1.

`Portland(config-route-map)#exit`	Returns to global configuration mode.
`Portland(config)#route-map 172To192 permit 10`	Creates a route map named 172To192.
`Portland(config-route-map)#match ip address 102`	Specifies the match criteria— match addresses filtered from ACL 102.
`Portland(config-route-map)#set interface fastethernet 0/0`	Specifies the set actions—forward packets out interface fastethernet 0/0.
`Portland(config-route-map)#exit`	Returns to global configuration mode.
`Portland(config)#interface serial 0/0`	Moves to interface configuration mode.
`Portland(config-if)#description link to ISP1`	Sets a locally significant description of the interface.
`Portland(config-if)#ip address 198.133.219.1 255.255.255.252`	Assigns an IP address and netmask.
`Portland(config-if)#no shutdown`	Enables the interface.
`Portland(config)#interface serial 0/1`	Moves to interface configuration mode.
`Portland(config-if)#description link to ISP2`	Sets a locally significant description of the interface.
`Portland(config-if)#ip address 192.31.7.1 255.255.255.252`	Assigns an IP address and netmask.
`Portland(config-if)#no shutdown`	Enables the interface.
`Portland(config)#interface fastethernet 0/0`	Moves to interface configuration mode.
`Portland(config-if)#ip address 192.168.1.1 255.255.255.0`	Configures an IP address and netmask.
`Portland(config-if)#ip policy route-map ISP1`	Applies the route map named ISP1 to this interface.

Portland(config-if)#**ip policy route-map 192To172**	Applies the route map named 192To172 to this interface.
Portland(config-if)#**no shutdown**	Enables the interface.
Portland(config-if)#**exit**	Returns to global configuration mode.
Portland(config)#**interface fastethernet 0/1**	Moves to interface configuration mode.
Portland(config-if)#**ip address 172.16.1.1 255.255.255.0**	Configures an IP address and netmask.
Portland(config-if)#**ip policy route-map ISP2**	Applies the route map named ISP2 to this interface.
Portland(config-if)#**ip policy route-map 172To192**	Applies the route map named 172To192 to this interface.
Portland(config-if)#**no shutdown**	Enables the interface.
Portland(config-if)#**exit**	Returns to global configuration mode.
Portland(config)#**exit**	Returns to privileged mode.
Portland#**copy running-config startup-config**	Saves the configuration to NVRAM.

Administrative Distance (AD)

The Cisco default administrative distances are as follows:

Route Source	AD
Connected interface	0
Static route	1
EIGRP summary route	5
External Border Gateway Protocol (BGP)	20
EIGRP	90
Interior Gateway Routing Protocol (IGRP)	100

Route Source	AD
OSPF	110
IS-IS	115
RIP	120
Exterior Gateway Protocol (EGP)	140
External EIGRP	170
Internal BGP	200
Unknown	255

NOTE: If a static route refers to an exit interface rather than a next-hop address, the destination is considered to be directly connected, and therefore given an AD of 0 rather than 1.

Router(config)#**router ospf 1**	Starts the OSPF routing process.
Router(config-router)#**distance 95**	Changes the AD of OSPF from 110 to 95.
Router(config-router)#**distance 105 192.168.10.2 0.0.0.0**	Applies an AD of 105 to all OSPF routes received from 192.169.10.2.
	NOTE: This newly assigned AD is locally significant only. All other routers will still apply an AD of 110 to these routes.
Router(config)#**router ospf 1**	Starts the OSPF routing process.
Router(config-router)#**distance 105 172.16.10.2 0.0.0.0**	Applies an AD of 105 to all OSPF routes received from 172.16.10.2.
Router(config-router)#**distance 95 172.16.20.2 0.0.0.0 2**	Assigns an AD of 95 to any routes matching ACL 2 that are learned from 172.16.20.2.
Router(config-router)#**exit**	Leaves router configuration mode.
Router(config)#**access-list 2 permit 192.168.30.0 0.0.0.255**	Creates an ACL that will define what route or routes will have an AD of 95 assigned to it.

	NOTE: A named ACL can also be used. Replace the ACL number with the name of the ACL in this command: `Router(config-router)# distance 95 172.16.20.2 255.255.255.0 namedACL`

Static Routes: permanent Keyword

`Router(config)#ip route 192.168.50.0 255.255.255.0 serial 0/0 permanent`	Creates a static route that will not be removed from the routing table, even if the interface shuts down for any reason.

TIP: Without the **permanent** keyword in a static route statement, a static route will be removed if an interface goes down. A downed interface will cause the directly connected network and any associated static routes to be removed from the routing table. If the interface comes back up, the routes will be returned.

Adding the **permanent** keyword to a static route statement will keep the static routes in the routing table even if the interface goes down and the directly connected networks are removed. You *cannot* get to these routes—the interface is down—but the routes remain in the table. The advantage to this is that when the interface comes back up, the static routes do not need to be reprocessed and placed back into the routing table, saving time and processing power.

When a static route is added or deleted, this route, along with all other static routes, is processed in one second. Before Cisco IOS Software Release 12.0, this was five seconds.

The routing table processes static routes every minute to install or remove static routes according to the changing routing table.

Floating Static Routes

`Router(config)#ip route 192.168.50.0 255.255.255.0 s0/0 130`	Creates a static route that has an AD of 130 rather than the default AD of 1.

TIP: By default, a static route will always be used rather than a routing protocol. By adding an AD number to your **ip route** statement, you can effectively create a backup route to your routing protocol. If your network is using EIGRP, and you need a backup the route, add a static route with an AD greater than 90. EIGRP will be used because its AD is better (lower) than the static route. If EIGRP goes down, the static route is used in its place. When EIGRP is running again, EIGRP routes are used because their AD will again be lower than the AD of the floating static route.

Static Routes and Recursive Lookups

A static route that uses a next-hop address (intermediate address) will cause the router to look at the routing table twice: once when a packet first enters the router and the router looks up the entry in the table, and a second time when the router has to resolve the location of the intermediate address.

For point-to-point links, always use an exit interface in your static route statements:

```
Router(config)#ip route 192.168.10.0 255.255.255.0 s0/0
```

For broadcast links such as Ethernet or Fast Ethernet, use *both* an exit interface and intermediate address:

```
Router(config)#ip route 192.168.10.0 255.255.255.0 fa0/0
192.138.20.2
```

This saves the router from having to do a recursive lookup for the intermediate address of 192.168.20.2, knowing that the exit interface is FastEthernet 0/0.

Try to avoid using static routes that reference only intermediate addresses.

DHCP Configuration

`Router(config)#ip dhcp pool internal`	Creates a DHCP pool called internal.
`Router(dhcp-config)#network` `172.16.10.0 255.255.255.0`	Defines the range of addresses to be leased.
`Router(dhcp-config)#default-router` `172.16.10.1`	Defines the address of the default router for the client.
`Router(dhcp-config)#dns-server` `172.16.10.10`	Defines the address of the Domain Name System (DNS) server for the client.
`Router(dhcp-config)#netbios-name-` `server 172.16.10.10`	Defines the address of the NetBIOS server for the client.
`Router(dhcp-config)#domain-name` `fakedomainname.ca`	Defines the domain name for the client.
`Router(dhcp-config)#lease 14 12 23`	Defines the lease time to be 14 days, 12 hours, 23 minutes.
`Router(dhcp-config)#lease infinite`	Sets the lease time to infinity (default, 1 day).

`Router(dhcp-config)#exit`	Returns to global configuration mode.
`Router(config)#ip dhcp excluded-address 172.16.10.1 172.16.10.9`	Specifies the range of addresses not to be leased out to clients.
`Router(config)#service dhcp`	Enables the DHCP service and relay features on a Cisco IOS router.
`Router(config)#no service dhcp`	Turns the DHCP service off. The DHCP service is on by default in Cisco IOS Software.

Verifying and Troubleshooting DHCP Configuration

`Router#show ip dhcp binding`	Displays a list of all bindings created.
`Router#show ip dhcp binding w.x.y.z`	Displays the bindings for a specific DHCP client with an IP address of w.x.y.z.
`Router#clear ip dhcp binding a.b.c.d`	Clears an automatic address binding from the DHCP server database.
`Router#clear ip dhcp binding *`	Clears all automatic DHCP bindings.
`Router#show ip dhcp conflict`	Displays a list of all address conflicts recorded by the DHCP server.
`Router#clear ip dhcp conflict a.b.c.d`	Clears an address conflict from the database.
`Router#clear ip dhcp conflict *`	Clears conflicts for all addresses.
`Router#show ip dhcp database`	Displays any recent activity on the DHCP database.
`Router#show ip dhcp server statistics`	Displays a list of the number of messages sent and received by the DHCP server.
`Router#clear ip dhcp server statistics`	Resets all DHCP server counters to 0.
`Router#debug ip dhcp server {events | packets | linkage | class}`	Displays the DHCP process of addresses being leased and returned.

Configuring a DHCP Helper Address

Router(config)#**interface fastethernet 0/0**	Moves to interface configuration mode.
Router(config-if)#**ip helper-address 172.16.20.2**	DHCP broadcasts will be forwarded as a unicast to this specific address instead of being dropped by the router.

NOTE: The use of the **ip helper-address** command will forward broadcast packets as a unicast to eight different UDP ports by default:

- TFTP (port 69)
- DNS (port 53)
- Time service (port 37)
- NetBIOS Name Server (port 137)
- NetBIOS Datagram Server (port 138)
- Boot Protocol (BOOTP) client and server datagrams (ports 67 and 68)
- TACACS service (port 49)

NOTE: If you want to close some of these ports, use the **no ip forward-protocol udp** *x* command at the global configuration prompt, where *x* is the port number you want to close. The following command stops the forwarding of broadcasts to port 49:

Router(config)#**no ip forward-protocol udp 49**

NOTE: If you want to open other UDP ports, use the **ip forward-helper udp** *x* command, where *x* is the port number you want to open:

Router(config)#**ip forward-protocol udp 517**

DHCP Client on a Cisco IOS Ethernet Interface

Router(config)#**interface fastethernet 0/0**	Moves to interface configuration mode.
Router(config-if)#**ip address dhcp**	Specifies that the interface acquire an IP address through DHCP.

Configuration Example: DHCP

Figure 5-4 shows the network topology for the configuration that follows, which demostrates how to configure DHCP services on a Cisco IOS router using the commands covered in this chapter.

Figure 5-4   Network Topology for DHCP Configuration

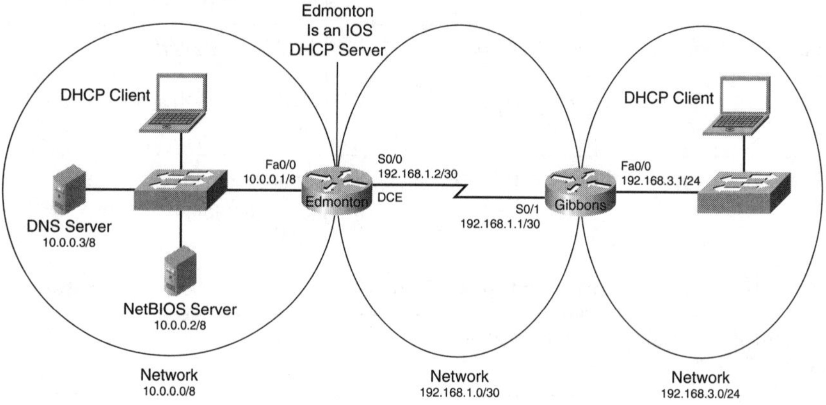

Edmonton Router

router>**enable**	Moves to privileged mode.
router#**configure terminal**	Moves to global configuration mode.
router(config)#**host Edmonton**	Sets the host name.
Edmonton(config)#**interface fastethernet 0/0**	Moves to interface configuration mode.
Edmonton(config-if)#**description LAN Interface**	Sets a local description of the interface.
Edmonton(config-if)#**ip address 10.0.0.1 255.0.0.0**	Assigns an IP address and netmask.
Edmonton(config-if)#**no shutdown**	Enables the interface.
Edmonton(config-if)#**interface serial 0/0**	Moves to interface configuration mode.

`Edmonton(config-if)#`**`description link to`** **`Gibbons Router`**	Sets a local description of the interface.
`Edmonton(config-if)#`**`ip address`** **`192.168.1.2 255.255.255.252`**	Assigns an IP address and netmask.
`Edmonton(config-if)#`**`clock rate 56000`**	Assigns the clock rate to the DCE cable on this side of the link.
`Edmonton(config-if)#`**`no shutdown`**	Enables the interface.
`Edmonton(config-if)#`**`exit`**	Returns to global configuration mode.
`Edmonton(config)#`**`router eigrp 10rip`**	Enables the EIGRP routing process for autonomous system 10.
`Edmonton(config-router)#`**`network 10.0.0.0`**	Advertises the 10.0.0.0 network.
`Edmonton(config-router)#`**`network`** **`192.168.1.0`**	Advertises the 192.168.1.0 network.
`Edmonton(config-router)#`**`exit`**	Returns to global configuration mode.
`Edmonton(config)#`**`service dhcp`**	Verifies that the router can use DHCP services and that DHCP is enabled.
`Edmonton(config)#`**`ip dhcp pool 10network`**	Creates a DHCP pool called 10network.
`Edmonton(dhcp-config)#`**`network 10.0.0.0`** **`255.0.0.0`**	Defines the range of addresses to be leased.
`Edmonton(dhcp-config)#`**`default-router`** **`10.0.0.1`**	Defines the address of the default router for clients.
`Edmonton(dhcp-config)#`**`netbios-name-server`** **`10.0.0.2`**	Defines the address of the NetBIOS server for clients.
`Edmonton(dhcp-config)#`**`dns-server 10.0.0.3`**	Defines the address of the DNS server for clients.
`Edmonton(dhcp-config)#`**`domain-name`** **`fakedomainname.ca`**	Defines the domain name for clients.

Edmonton(dhcp-config)#**lease 12 14 30**	Set the lease time to be 12 days, 14 hours, 30 minutes.
Edmonton(dhcp-config)#**exit**	Returns to global configuration mode.
Edmonton(config)#**ip dhcp excluded-address 10.0.0.1 10.0.0.5**	Specifies the range of addresses not to be leased out to clients.
Edmonton(config)#**ip dhcp pool 192.168.3network**	Creates a DHCP pool called 192.168.3network.
Edmonton(dhcp-config)#**network 192.168.3.0 255.255.255.0**	Defines a range of addresses to be leased.
Edmonton(dhcp-config)#**default-router 192.168.3.1**	Defines the address of the default router for clients.
Edmonton(dhcp-config)#**netbios-name-server 10.0.0.2**	Defines the address of the NetBIOS server for clients.
Edmonton(dhcp-config)#**dns-server 10.0.0.3**	Defines the address of the DNS server for clients.
Edmonton(dhcp-config)#**domain-name fakedomainname.ca**	Defines the domain name for clients.
Edmonton(dhcp-config)#**lease 12 14 30**	Sets the lease time to be 12 days, 14 hours, 30 minutes.
Edmonton(dhcp-config)#**exit**	Returns to global configuration mode.
Edmonton(config)#**exit**	Returns to privileged mode.
Edmonton#**copy running-config startup-config**	Saves the configuration to NVRAM.

Gibbons Router

router>**enable**	Moves to privileged mode.
router#**configure terminal**	Moves to global configuration mode.
router(config)#**host Gibbons**	Sets the host name.

`Gibbons(config)#interface fastethernet 0/0`	Moves to interface configuration mode.
`Gibbons(config-if)#description LAN Interface`	Sets a local description of the interface.
`Gibbons(config-if)#ip address 192.168.3.1 255.255.255.0`	Assigns an IP address and netmask.
`Gibbons(config-if)#ip helper-address 192.168.1.2`	DHCP broadcasts will be forwarded as a unicast to this address instead of being dropped.
`Gibbons(config-if)#no shutdown`	Enables the interface.
`Gibbons(config-if)#interface serial 0/1`	Moves to interface configuration mode.
`Gibbons(config-if)#description link to Edmonton Router`	Sets a local description of the interface.
`Gibbons(config-if)#ip address 192.168.1.1 255.255.255.252`	Assigns an IP address and netmask.
`Gibbons(config-if)#no shutdown`	Enables the interface.
`Gibbons(config-if)#exit`	Returns to global configuration mode.
`Gibbons(config)#router eigrp 10`	Enables the EIGRP routing process for autonomous system 10.
`Gibbons(config-router)#network 192.168.3.0`	Advertises the 192.168.3.0 network.
`Gibbons(config-router)#network 192.168.1.0`	Advertises the 192.168.1.0 network.
`Gibbons(config-router)#exit`	Returns to global configuration mode.
`Gibbons(config)#exit`	Returns to privileged mode.
`Gibbons#copy running-config startup-config`	Saves the configuration to NVRAM.

CHAPTER 6

BGP

This chapter provides information and commands concerning the following Border Gateway Protocol (BGP) topics:

- Configuring BGP
- BGP and loopback addresses
- eBGP multihop
- Verifying BGP connections
- Troubleshooting BGP connections
- Autonomous system synchronization
- Default routes
- Load balancing
- Authentication
- Attributes
  - Origin
  - Next hop
  - Autonomous system path: Remove private autonomous system
  - Autonomous system path: Prepend
  - Weight: The **weight** command
  - Weight: Access lists
  - Weight: Route maps
  - Local preference: **bgp default local-preference** command
  - Local preference: Route maps
  - Multi-Exit Discriminator (MED)
  - Atomic aggregate
- Regular expressions
  - Regular expressions: Example one
  - Regular expressions: Example two
- BGP route filtering using access lists
- BGP route filtering using prefix lists
- BGP: Configuration example

Configuring BGP

`Router(config)#router bgp 100`	Starts BGP routing process 100.
	NOTE: Cisco IOS Software permits only one BGP process to run at a time; therefore, a router cannot belong to more than one autonomous system.
`Router(config-router)#network 192.135.250.0`	Tells the BGP process what locally learned networks to advertise.
	NOTE: The networks can be connected routes, static routes, or routes learned via a dynamic routing protocol, such as Open Shortest Path First (OSPF).
	NOTE: Configuring just a network statement will *not* establish a BGP neighbor relationship.
	NOTE: The networks must also exist in the local router's routing table; otherwise, they will not be sent out in updates.
`Router(config-router)#network 128.107.0.0 mask 255.255.255.0`	Used to specify an individual subnet.
	TIP: Routes learned by the BGP process are propagated by default but are often filtered by a routing policy.
`Router(config-router)#neighbor 192.31.7.1 remote-as 200`	Identifies a peer router with which this router will establish a BGP session. The autonomous system number will determine whether the neighbor router is an eBGP or iBGP neighbor.
	TIP: If the autonomous system number configured in the **router bgp** command is identical to the autonomous system number configured in the **neighbor** statement, BGP initiates an internal session—iBGP. If the field values differ, BGP builds an external session—eBGP.
`Router(config-router)#neighbor 24.1.1.2 shutdown`	Disables the active session between the local router and 24.1.1.2.
`Router(config-router)timers bgp 90 240`	Changes the BGP network timers. The first number is the keepalive timer (default, 60 seconds). The second number is the holdtime timer (default, 180 seconds).

BGP and Loopback Addresses

`Router(config)#`**`router bgp 100`**	Starts the BGP routing process.
`Router(config-router)#`**`neighbor 172.16.1.2 update-source loopback 0`**	Informs the router to use any operational interface for TCP connections (in this case, Loopback 0). Because a loopback interface never goes down, this adds more stability to your configuration as compared to using a physical interface.
	TIP: Without the **neighbor update-source** command, BGP will use the closest IP interface to the peer. This command provides BGP with a more robust configuration, because BGP will still operate in the event the link to the closest interface fails.
	NOTE: You can use the **neighbor update-source** command with either eBGP or iBGP sessions. In the case of a point-to-point eBGP session, this command is not needed because there is only one path for BGP to use.

eBGP Multihop

Figure 6-1 shows commands necessary to configure eBGP multihop.

Figure 6-1   *Network Topology for eBGP Multihop Configuration*

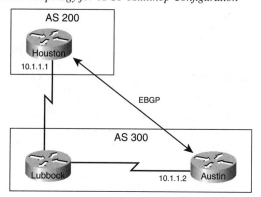

`Houston(config)#router bgp 200`	Starts the BGP routing process.
`Houston(config-router)#neighbor 10.1.1.2 remote-as 300`	Identifies a peer router at 10.1.1.2.
`Houston(config-router)#neighbor 10.1.1.2 ebgp-multihop 2`	Allows for two routers that are not directly connected to establish an eBGP session.
`Austin(config)#router bgp 300`	Starts the BGP routing process.
`Austin(config-router)#neighbor 10.1.1.1 remote-as 200`	Identifies a peer router at 10.1.1.1.
`Austin(config-router)#neighbor 10.1.1.1 ebgp-multihop 2`	Allows for two routers that are not directly connected to establish an eBGP session.

NOTE: The **ebgp-multihop** keyword is a Cisco IOS option. It must be configured on each peer. The **ebgp-multihop** keyword is only used for eBGP sessions, not for iBGP.

eBGP neighbors are usually directly connected (over a WAN connection, for example) to establish an eBGP session. However, sometimes one of the directly connected routers is unable to run BGP. The **ebgp-multihop** keyword allows for a logical connection to be made between peer routers, even if they are not directly connected. The **ebgp-multihop** keyword allows for an eBGP peer to be up to 255 hops away and still create an eBGP session.

Verifying BGP Connections

`Router#show ip bgp`	Displays entries in the BGP routing table.
`Router#show ip bgp neighbors`	Displays information about the BGP and TCP connections to neighbors.
`Router#show ip bgp summary`	Displays the status of all BGP connections.

Troubleshooting BGP Connections

`Router#clear ip bgp *`	Forces BGP to clear its table and resets all BGP sessions.

`Router#clear ip bgp 10.1.1.1`	Resets the specific BGP session with the neighbor at 10.1.1.1.
`Router#debug ip bgp`	Displays information related to processing BGP.

CAUTION: The **clear ip bgp *** command is both processor and memory intensive and should be used only in smaller environments. A more reasonable approach is to clear only a specific network or a specific session with a neighbor with the **clear ip bgp** *specific-network* command. However, you can use this command whenever the following changes occur:

- Additions or changes to the BGP-related access lists
- Changes to BGP-related weights
- Changes to BGP-related distribution lists
- Changes in the BGP timer's specifications
- Changes to the BGP administrative distance
- Changes to BGP-related route maps

Autonomous System Synchronization

`Router(config)#router bgp 100`	Starts the BGP routing process.
`Router(config-router)#synchronization`	Enables synchronization.

NOTE: The BGP synchronization rule states that a BGP router should not advertise to external neighbors destinations learned from inside BGP neighbors unless those destinations are also known via an IGP.

NOTE: By default, synchronization between BGP and the IGP is turned off to allow the Cisco IOS Software to advertise a network route without waiting for route validation from the IGP. This feature allows routers and access servers within an autonomous system to have the route before BGP makes it available to other autonomous systems.

Use the **synchronization** command if routers in the autonomous system do not speak BGP.

`Router(config-router)#no synchronization`	Overrides the BGP synchronization requirement.

NOTE: The **no synchronization** command is a Cisco-only command.

TIP: In two situations, you can safely turn off synchronization:

- When all transit routers inside the autonomous system are running fully meshed iBGP
- When the autonomous system is not a transit autonomous system

Default Routes

`Router(config)#router bgp 100`	Starts the BGP routing process.
`Router(config-router)#neighbor 192.168.100.1 remote-as 200`	Identifies a peer router at 192.168.100.1.
`Router(config-router)#neighbor 192.168.100.1 default-originate`	The default route of 0.0.0.0 will only be sent to 192.168.100.1.

NOTE: If you want your BGP router to advertise a default to all peers, use the **network** command with an address of 0.0.0.0:

`RTC(config)#router bgp 100`

`RTC(config-router)#neighbor 172.16.20.1 remote-as 150`

`RTC(config-router)#neighbor 172.17.1.1 remote-as 200`

`RTC(config-router)#network 0.0.0.0`

Load Balancing

`Router(config)#router bgp 100`	Starts the BGP routing process.
`Router(config-router)#maximum-paths 3`	Enables BGP load balancing over 3 equal-cost paths.
`Router(config-router)#maximum-paths ibgp 3`	Enables BGP load balancing over 3 equal-cost iBGP paths.
`Router(config-router)#maximum-paths eibgp 3`	Enables BGP load balancing for 3 equal-cost eBGP and iBGP paths.

NOTE: BGP supports a maximum of 16 paths per destination, but only if they are sourced from the same autonomous system. By default, BGP installs only one path to the IP routing table.

Authentication

Router(config)#**router bgp 100**	Starts the BGP routing process.
Router(config-router)#**neighbor 198.133.219.1 password tower**	Specifies that the router and its peer at 198.133.219.1 use Message Digest 5 (MD5) authentication on the TCP connection between them.

NOTE: The password must be the same on both BGP peers. The password is case sensitive and can be up to 25 alphanumeric characters when the **service password-encryption** command is enabled and up to 81 characters when the **service password-encryption** command is not enabled. The first character cannot be a number. The string can contain any alphanumeric characters, including spaces. You cannot specify a password in the format *number-space-anything*. The space after the number can cause authentication to fail.

Attributes

Routes learned via BGP have associated properties that are used to determine the best route to a destination when multiple paths exist to a particular destination. These properties are referred to as *BGP attributes*, and an understanding of how BGP attributes influence route selection is required for the design of robust networks. This section describes the attributes that BGP uses in the route selection process.

Origin

The *origin attribute* indicates how BGP learned about a particular route.

Router(config)#**route-map SETORIGIN permit 10**	Creates a route map called SETORIGIN. This route map will permit traffic based on subsequent criteria. A sequence number of 10 is assigned.
	NOTE: The *sequence-number* is used to indicate what position the route map is to have in a list of route maps configured with the same name. If no sequence number is given, the first condition in the route map is automatically numbered as 10.
Router(config-route-map)#**match as-path 10**	Specifies the condition under which redistribution or policy routing is allowed. In this case, it must match routes from autonomous system path 10.

Router(config-route-map)#**set origin igp**	Sets the origin code of the routing update as IGP.
Router(config-route-map)#**exit**	Returns to global configuration mode.
Router(config)#**router bgp 100**	Starts the BGP routing process.
Router(config-router)#**redistribute eigrp 51 route-map SETORIGIN**	Redistributes EIGRP autonomous system 51 into BGP using the route map called SETORIGIN as the conditions for redistribution.

NOTE: The three options for the origin attribute in the **set origin** command are **igp**, **egp**, and **incomplete**.

Next Hop

The eBGP next-hop attribute is the IP address that is used to reach the advertising router. For eBGP peers, the next-hop address is the IP address of the connection between the peers. For iBGP, the eBGP next-hop address is carried into the local autonomous system.

Figure 6-2 shows commands necessary to configure the next-hop attribute.

Figure 6-2   Network Topology for Next-Hop Attribute Configuration

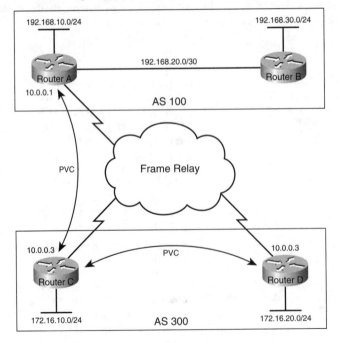

`RouterC(config)#`**`router bgp 300`**	Starts the BGP routing process.
`RouterC(config-router)#`**`neighbor 10.0.0.1 remote-as 100`**	Identifies a peer router at 10.0.0.1.
`RouterC(config-router)#`**`neighbor 10.0.0.1 next-hop-self`**	Forces all updates destined to the neighbor at 10.0.0.1 to advertise this router as the next hop.
	NOTE: Router C advertises 172.16.20.0 to Router A with a next hop of 10.0.0.3, just as it would do if the common media were Ethernet. The problem is that Router A does not have a direct permanent virtual connection (PVC) to Router D and cannot reach the next hop, so routing will fail. To remedy this situation, use the **neighbor next-hop-self** router configuration command. The **neighbor next-hop-self** command causes Router C to advertise 172.16.20.0 with the next-hop attribute set to 10.0.0.3.
	TIP: This command proves useful in nonmeshed networks (such as Frame Relay or X.25) where BGP neighbors might not have direct access to all other neighbors on the same IP subnet.
`RouterC(config-router)#`**`neighbor 10.0.0.1 next-hop-unchanged`**	Enables an eBGP multihop peer to propagate the next hop unchanged.
	WARNING: This command should not be configured on a route reflector, and the **neighbor next-hop-self** command should not be used to modify the next-hop attribute for a route reflector when this feature is enabled for a route reflector client.
	Route reflectors are a solution for dealing with iBGP peering within an autonomous system. Route reflectors allow a router to advertise (reflect) iBGP-learned routes to other iBGP routers, thereby reducing the number of iBGP peers within an autonomous system.

Autonomous System Path: Remove Private Autonomous System

Private autonomous system numbers (64,512 to 65,535) cannot be passed on to the Internet because they are not unique. Cisco has implemented a feature, **remove-private-as**, to strip private autonomous system numbers out of the AS_PATH list before the routes get propagated to the Internet.

Figure 6-3 shows commands necessary to configure the **remove-private-as** option.

Figure 6-3   Network Topology for Remote Private Autonomous System Configuration

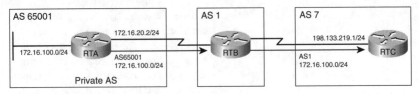

RouterB(config)#**router bgp 1**	Starts the BGP routing process.
RouterB(config-router)#**neighbor 172.16.20.2 remote-as 65001**	Identifies a peer router at 172.16.20.2.
RouterB(config-router)#**neighbor 198.133.219.1 remote-as 7**	Identifies a peer router at 198.133.219.1.
RouterB(config-router)#**neighbor 198.133.219.1 remove-private-as**	Removes private autonomous system numbers from the path in outbound routing updates.
	NOTE: The **remove-private-as** command is available for EBGP neighbors only.

Autonomous System Path: Prepend

You can influence the decision-making process with regard to the AS_PATH attribute by prepending, or adding, extra autonomous system numbers to the AS_PATH attribute. Assuming that the values of all other attributes are the same, routers will pick the shortest AS_PATH attribute; therefore, prepending numbers to the path will manipulate the decision as to the best path.

Figure 6-4 shows commands necessary to configure the **as-path prepend** option.

Figure 6-4   Network Topology for AS_PATH Prepend Configuration

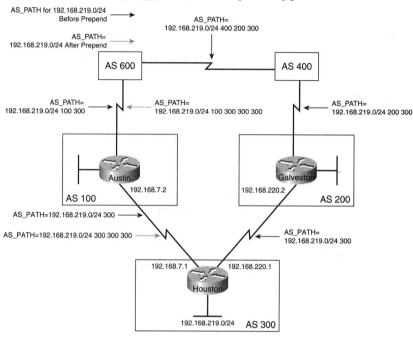

In this scenario, you want to use the configuration of Houston to influence the choice of paths in autonomous system 600. Currently, the routers in autonomous system 600 have reachability information to the 192.168.219.0/24 network via two routes: via autonomous system 100 with an AS_PATH attribute of (100, 300) and via autonomous system 400 with an AS_PATH attribute of (400, 200, 300). Assuming that the values of all other attributes are the same, the routers in autonomous system 600 will pick the shortest AS_PATH attribute: the route through autonomous system 100. You will prepend, or add, extra autonomous system numbers to the AS_PATH attribute for routes that Houston advertises to autonomous system 100 to have autonomous system 600 select autonomous system 400 as the preferred path of reaching the 192.168.219.0/24 network.

Houston(config)#**router bgp 300**	Starts the BGP routing process.
Houston(config-router)#**network 192.168.219.0**	Tells the BGP process what locally learned networks to advertise.
Houston(config-router)#**neighbor 192.168.220.2 remote-as 200**	Identifies a peer router at 192.168.220.2.
Houston(config-router)#**neighbor 192.168.7.2 remote-as 100**	Identifies a peer router at 192.168.7.2.
Houston(config-router)#**neighbor 192.168.7.2 route-map SETPATH out**	All routes destined for 192.168.7.2 will have to follow the conditions laid out by the SETPATH route map.

Houston(config-router)#exit	Moves to global configuration mode.
Houston(config)#route-map SETPATH permit 10	Creates a route map named SETPATH. This route map will permit traffic based on subsequent criteria. A sequence number of 10 is assigned.
Houston(config-route-map)#set as-path prepend 300 300	The local router will add (prepend) the autonomous system number 300 twice to the AS_PATH attribute before sending it out to its neighbor at 192.168.7.2.

The result of this configuration is that the AS_PATH attribute of updates for network 192.168.219.0 that autonomous system 600 receives via autonomous system 100 will be (100, 300, 300, 300), which is longer than the value of the AS_PATH attribute of updates for network 192.168.219.0 that autonomous system 600 receives via autonomous system 400 (400, 200, 300).

Autonomous system 600 will choose autonomous system 400 (400, 200, 300) as the better path. This is because BGP is a path vector routing protocol that chooses the path with the least number of autonomous systems that it has to cross.

Weight: The weight Command

The **weight** attribute is a special Cisco attribute that is used in the path selection process when there is more than one route to the same destination.

Figure 6-5 shows commands necessary to configure the **weight** attribute.

Figure 6-5   Network Topology for Weight Attribute Configuration

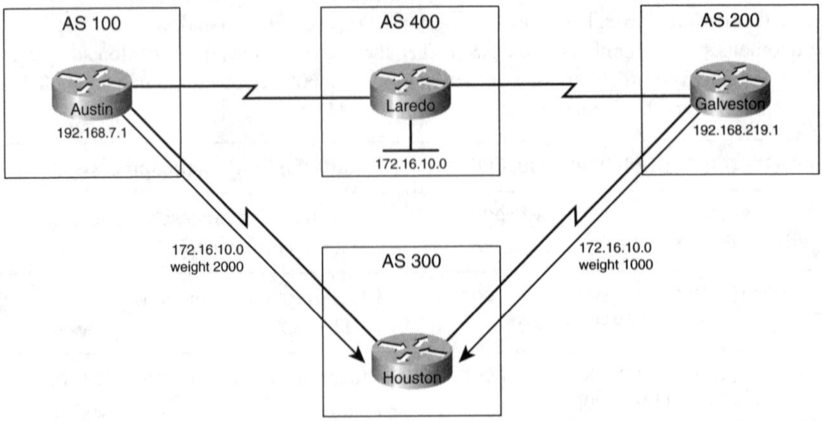

Houston(config)#router bgp 300	Starts the BGP routing process.
Houston(config-router)#neighbor 192.168.7.1 remote-as 100	Identifies a peer router at 192.168.7.1.
Houston(config-router)#neighbor 192.168.7.1 weight 2000	Sets the weight of all route updates from autonomous system 100 to 2000.
Houston(config-router)#neighbor 192.168.219.1 remote-as 200	Identifies a peer router at 192.168.219.1.
Houston(config-router)#neighbor 192.168.219.1 weight 1000	Sets the weight of all route updates from autonomous system 200 to 1000.

The result of this configuration will have Houston accept the 172.16.10.0 network from autonomous system 100, because it has a higher **weight** attribute set as compared to autonomous system 200.

> **NOTE:**   The **weight** attribute is local to the router and *not propagated* to other routers. By default, the weight attribute is 32,768 for paths that the router originates, and zero for other paths. Routes with a *higher weight are preferred* when there are multiple routes to the same destination.

Weight: Access Lists

Refer back to Figure 6-5 to see commands necessary to configure the **weight** attribute using access lists.

Houston(config)#router bgp 300	Starts the BGP routing process.
Houston(config-router)#neighbor 192.168.7.1 remote-as 100	Identifies a peer router at 192.168.7.1.
Houston(config-router)#neighbor 192.168.7.1 filter-list 5 weight 2000	Assigns a **weight** attribute of 2000 to updates from the neighbor at 192.168.7.1 that are permitted by access list 5. Access list 5 is defined in the **ip as-path access-list 5** command listed below in global configuration mode. Filter list 5 refers to the **ip as-path access-list 5** command that defines which path will be used to have this weight value assigned to it.

Houston(config-router)#**neighbor 192.168.219.1 remote-as 200**	Identifies a peer router at 192.168.219.1.
Houston(config-router)#**neighbor 192.168.219.1 filter-list 6 weight 1000**	Assigns a **weight** attribute of 1000 to updates from the neighbor at 192.168.219.1 that are permitted by access list 6. Access list 6 is defined in the **ip as-path access-list 5** command listed below in global configuration mode.
Houston(config-router)#**exit**	Returns to global configuration mode.
Houston(config)#**ip as-path access-list 5 permit ^100$**	Permits updates whose AS_PATH attribute starts with 100 (represented by the ^) and ends with 100 (represented by the $).
	The ^ and $ symbols are used to form regular expressions. See the section "Regular Expressions" in this chapter after the sections on the different attributes for more examples.
Houston(config)#**ip as-path access-list 6 permit ^200$**	Permits updates whose AS_PATH attribute starts with 200 (represented by the ^) and ends with 200 (represented by the $).

The result of this configuration will have Houston accept the 172.16.10.0 network from autonomous system 100, because it has a higher **weight** attribute set as compared to autonomous system 200.

Weight: Route Maps

Refer back to Figure 6-5 to see commands necessary to configure the **weight** attribute using route maps.

Houston(config)#**router bgp 300**	Starts the BGP routing process.
Houston(config-router)#**neighbor 192.168.7.1 remote-as 100**	Identifies a peer router at 192.168.7.1.
Houston(config-router)#**neighbor 192.168.7.1 route-map SETWEIGHT in**	The route map named SETWEIGHT will be used to assign weights to route updates.

`Houston(config-router)#`**`neighbor`** `192.168.219.1 remote-as 200`	Identifies a peer router at 192.168.219.1.
`Houston(config-router)#`**`neighbor`** `192.168.219.1 route-map SETWEIGHT in`	Identifies that the route map named SETWEIGHT will be used to assign weights to route updates.
`Houston(config-router)#`**`exit`**	Returns to global configuration mode.
`Houston(config)#`**`ip as-path`** **`access-list 5 permit ^100$`**	Permits updates whose AS_PATH attribute starts with 100 (represented by the ^) and ends with 100 (represented by the $).
`Houston(config)#`**`route-map`** **`SETWEIGHT permit 10`**	Creates a route map called SETWEIGHT. This route map will permit traffic based on subsequent criteria. A sequence number of 10 is assigned.
`Houston(config-route-map)#`**`match`** **`as-path 5`**	Specifies the condition under which policy routing is allowed—matching the BGP access control list (ACL) 5.
`Houston(config-route-map)#`**`set`** **`weight 2000`**	Assigns a weight of 2000 to any route update that meets the condition of ACL 5— an AS_PATH that starts with 100 and ends with 100.
`Houston(config-route-map)#`**`exit`**	Returns to global configuration mode.
`Houston(config)#`**`route-map`** **`SETWEIGHT permit 20`**	Creates the second statement for the route map named SETWEIGHT. This route map will permit traffic based on subsequent criteria. A sequence number of 20 is assigned.
`Houston(config-route-map)#`**`set`** **`weight 1000`**	Assigns a weight of 1000 to route updates from any other autonomous system aside from 100—autonomous system 100 will be assigned a weight of 2000 due to the first instance of the route map.

The result of this configuration will have Houston accept the 172.16.10.0 network from autonomous system 100, because it has a higher **weight** attribute set as compared to autonomous system 200.

Local Preference: bgp default local-preference Command

The local preference attribute is used to indicate the preferred path to a remote destination if there are multiple paths to that destination. The local preference attribute is part of the routing update, and unlike the **weight** attribute, it will be exchanged between routers in the same autonomous system.

Figure 6-6 shows the commands necessary to configure the **bgp default local-preference** command.

*Figure 6-6   Network Topology for **bgp default local-preference** Configuration*

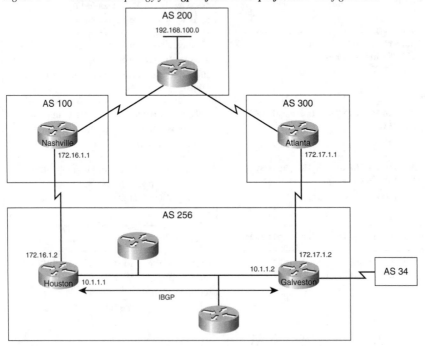

Houston(config)#**router bgp 256**	Starts the BGP routing process.
Houston(config-router)#**neighbor 172.16.1.1 remote-as 100**	Identifies a peer router at 172.16.1.1.
Houston(config-router)#**neighbor 10.1.1.2 remote-as 256**	Identifies a peer router at 10.1.1.2.
Houston(config-router)#**bgp default local-preference 150**	Sets the local preference attribute on this router.

Galveston(config)#`router bgp 256`	Starts the BGP routing process.
Galveston(config-router)#`neighbor 172.17.1.1 remote-as 300`	Identifies a peer router at 172.17.1.1.
Galveston(config-router)#`neighbor 10.1.1.1 remote-as 256`	Identifies a peer router at 10.1.1.1.
Galveston(config-router)#`bgp default local-preference 200`	Sets the local preference attribute on this router.

Based on these two configurations, traffic destined for a remote network that can be reached through autonomous system 256 will be routed through Galveston.

> **NOTE:** The **local-preference** value can be a number between 0 and 429,496,729. Higher is preferred. If a **local-preference** value is not set, the default is 100.

> **NOTE:** The **local-preference** attribute is local to the autonomous system—it is exchanged between iBGP peers but not advertised to eBGP peers. Use the **local-preference** attribute to force BGP routers to prefer one exit point over another.

Local Preference: Route Maps

Route maps provide more flexibility than the **bgp default local-preference** router configuration command.

Refer back to Figure 6-6 to see commands necessary to configure the **local-preference** attribute using route maps.

Galveston(config)#`router bgp 256`	Starts the BGP routing process.
Galveston(config-router)#`neighbor 172.17.1.1 remote-as 300`	Identifies a peer router at 172.17.1.1.
Galveston(config-router)#`neighbor 172.17.1.1 route-map SETLOCAL in`	Refers to a route map called SETLOCAL.
Galveston(config-router)#`neighbor 10.1.1.1 remote-as 256`	Identifies a peer router at 10.1.1.1.
Galveston(config-router)#`exit`	Returns to global configuration mode.
Galveston(config)#`ip as-path access-list 7 permit ^300$`	Permits updates whose AS_PATH attribute starts with 300 (represented by the ^) and ends with 300 (represented by the $).

`Galveston(config)#route-map SETLOCAL permit 10`	Creates a route map called SETLOCAL. This route map will permit traffic based on subsequent criteria. A sequence number of 10 is assigned.
`Galveston(config-route-map)#match as-path 7`	Specifies the condition under which policy routing is allowed—matching the BGP ACL 7.
`Galveston(config-route-map)#set local-preference 200`	Assigns a local preference of 200 to any update coming from autonomous system 300—as defined by ACL 7.
`Galveston(config-route-map)#route-map SETLOCAL permit 20`	Creates the second statement of the route map SETLOCAL. This instance will accept all other routes.

In the previous example, using the **bgp default local-preference** command on Galveston, the local preference attribute of *all* routing updates received by Galveston would be set to 200. This would include updates from autonomous system 34. In this example, using the **route-map** command, only updates received from autonomous system 300, as specified in the **ip as_path access-list** command, will have a local preference set to 200.

Multi-Exit Discriminator (MED)

The Multi-Exit Discriminator (MED) attribute provides a hint to external neighbors about which path to choose to an autonomous system that has multiple entry points.

Figure 6-7 shows the commands necessary to configure the MED attribute.

Figure 6-7   Network Topology for MED Attribute Configuration

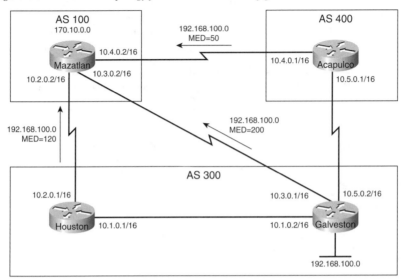

Mazatlan(config)#`router bgp 100`	Starts the BGP routing process.
Mazatlan(config-router)#`neighbor 10.2.0.1 remote-as 300`	Identifies a peer router at 10.2.0.1.
Mazatlan(config-router)#`neighbor 10.3.0.1 remote-as 300`	Identifies a peer router at 10.3.0.1.
Mazatlan(config-router)#`neighbor 10.4.0.1 remote-as 400`	Identifies a peer router at 10.4.0.1.
Acapulco(config)#`router bgp 400`	Starts the BGP routing process.
Acapulco(config-router)#`neighbor 10.4.0.2 remote-as 100`	Identifies a peer router at 10.4.0.2.
Acapulco(config-router)#`neighbor 10.4.0.2 route-map SETMEDOUT out`	Refers to a route map named SETMEDOUT.
Acapulco(config-router)#`neighbor 10.5.0.2 remote-as 300`	Identifies a peer router at 10.5.0.2.
Acapulco(config-router)#`exit`	Returns to global configuration mode.

`Acapulco(config)#route-map SETMEDOUT permit 10`	Creates a route map named SETMEDOUT. This route map will permit traffic based on subsequent criteria. A sequence number of 10 is assigned.
`Acapulco(config-route-map)#set metric 50`	Sets the metric value for BGP.
`Houston(config)#router bgp 300`	Starts the BGP routing process.
`Houston(config-router)#neighbor 10.2.0.1 remote-as 100`	Identifies a peer router at 10.2.0.1.
`Houston(config-router)#neighbor 10.2.0.1 route-map SETMEDOUT out`	Refers to a route map named SETMEDOUT.
`Houston(config-router)#neighbor 10.5.0.1 remote-as 400`	Identifies a peer router at 10.5.0.1.
`Houston(config-router)#neighbor 10.1.0.2 remote-as 300`	Identifies a peer router at 10.1.0.2.
`Houston(config-router)#exit`	Returns to global configuration mode.
`Houston(config)#route-map SETMEDOUT permit 10`	Creates a route map named SETMEDOUT. This route map will permit traffic based on subsequent criteria. A sequence number of 10 is assigned.
`Houston(config-route-map)#set metric 120`	Sets the metric value for BGP.
`Galveston(config)#router bgp 300`	Starts the BGP routing process.
`Galveston(config-router)#neighbor 10.3.0.2 remote-as 100`	Identifies a peer router at 10.3.0.2.
`Galveston(config-router)#neighbor 10.3.0.2 route-map SETMEDOUT out`	Refers to a route map named SETMEDOUT.
`Galveston(config-router)#neighbor 10.1.0.1 remote-as 300`	Identifies a peer router at 10.1.0.1.
`Galveston(config-router)#exit`	Returns to global configuration mode.

Galveston(config)#**route-map** **SETMEDOUT permit 10**	Creates a route map named SETMEDOUT. This route map will permit traffic based on subsequent criteria. A sequence number of 10 is assigned.
Galveston(config-route-map)#**set** **metric 200**	Sets the metric value for BGP.

- A lower MED value is preferred over a higher MED value. The default value of the MED is 0.
- Unlike local preference, the MED attribute is exchanged between autonomous systems, but an MED attribute that comes into an autonomous system does not leave the autonomous system.
- Unless otherwise specified, the router compares MED attributes for paths from external neighbors that are in the same autonomous system.
- If you want MED attributes from neighbors in other autonomous systems to be compared, you must configure the **bgp always-compare-med** command.

NOTE: By default, BGP compares the MED attributes of routes coming from neighbors in the same external autonomous system *as the route* (such as autonomous system 300). Mazatlan can only compare the MED attribute coming from Houston (120) to the MED attribute coming from Galveston (200) even though the update coming from Acapulco has the lowest MED value. Mazatlan will choose Houston as the best path for reaching network 192.168.100.0.

To force Mazatlan to include updates for network 192.168.100.0 from Acapulco in the comparison, use the **bgp always-compare-med** router configuration command on Mazatlan:

Mazatlan(config)#**router bgp 100**

Mazatlan(config-router)#**neighbor 10.2.0.1 remote-as 300**

Mazatlan(config-router)#**neighbor 10.3.0.1 remote-as 300**

Mazatlan(config-router)#**neighbor 10.4.0.1 remote-as 400**

Mazatlan(config-router)#**bgp always-compare-med**

Mazatlan will choose Acapulco as the best next hop for reaching network 192.168.100.0 assuming that all other attributes are the same.

Atomic Aggregate

A BGP router can transmit overlapping routes (nonidentical routes that point to the same destination) to another BGP router. When making a best path decision, a router always chooses the more specific path.

Figure 6-8 shows the commands necessary to configure the atomic aggregate attribute.

Figure 6-8   Network Topology for Atomic Aggregate Attribute Configuration

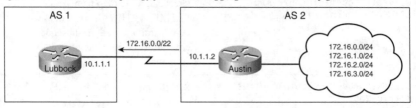

Lubbock(config)#**router bgp 1**	Starts the BGP routing process.
Lubbock(config-router)#**neighbor 10.1.1.2 remote-as 2**	Identifies a peer router at 10.1.1.2.
Austin(config)#**router bgp 2**	Starts the BGP routing process.
Austin(config-router)#**neighbor 10.1.1.1 remote-as 1**	Identifies a peer router at 10.1.1.1.
Austin(config-router)#**network 172.16.0.0 mask 255.255.255.0**	Advertises a specific subnet.
Austin(config-router)#**network 172.16.1.0 mask 255.255.255.0**	Advertises a specific subnet.
Austin(config-router)#**network 172.16.2.0 mask 255.255.255.0**	Advertises a specific subnet.
Austin(config-router)#**network 172.16.3.0 mask 255.255.255.0**	Advertises a specific subnet.
Austin(config-router)#**aggregate-address 172.16.0.0 255.255.252.0**	The aggregate address is now advertised.
	NOTE: To send the aggregate address, we only need one of the more specific routes configured. But by configuring all of them, the aggregate will be sent in case one of the networks goes down.

With this configuration, both Lubbock and Austin will have all the specific routes *and* the aggregate address in its BGP table—verify with **show ip bgp**:

```
Lubbock#show ip bgp 172.16.0.0 255.255.252.0

BGP routing table entry for 172.16.0.0/22, version 18
Paths: (1 available, best #1)
<text omitted>
 Origin IGP, localpref 100, valid, external, atomic- aggregate, best
```

Regular Expressions

A *regular expression* is a pattern to match against an input string, such as those listed in the following table.

Character	Description
^	Matches the beginning of the input string.
$	Matches the end of the input string.
_	Matches a space, comma, left brace, right brace, the beginning of an input string, or the ending of an input stream.
.	Matches any single character.
*	Matches 0 or more single- or multiple-character patterns.

For example, in the case of the **ip as-path access-list** command, the input string is the AS_PATH attribute.

`Router(config)#ip as-path access-list 1 permit 2150`	Will match any AS_PATH that includes the pattern of 2150.
`Router#show ip bgp regexp 2150`	Will match any AS_PATH that includes the pattern of 2150.
	NOTE: In both of these commands, not only will autonomous system 2150 be a match, but so will autonomous system 12150 or 21507.
`Router(config)#ip as-path access-list 6 deny ^200$`	Denies updates whose AS_PATH attribute starts with 200 (represented by the ^) and ends with 200 (represented by the $).
`Router(config)#ip as-path access-list 1 permit .*`	The period (.) symbol means any character, and the asterisk (*) symbol means a repetition of that character.
	NOTE: The argument of .* will match any value of the AS_PATH attribute.

Regular Expressions: Example One

Use the following output of the **show ip bgp** command to see how different examples of regular expressions can help filter specific patterns.

```
Router#show ip bgp

   Network              Next Hop             Metric LocPrf Weight Path
*> 10.0.0.0             0.0.0.0                   0           32768 i
*> 172.16.0.0           200.200.200.65            0     300    200  i
*> 192.168.2.0          200.200.200.65            0    0       300  i
```

```
Router# show ip bgp regexp ^300
```

- Match beginning of input string, AS_PATH, = 300.
- Last prepended autonomous system was 300.
- Routes matched: 172.16.0.0 and 192.168.20.0.

```
Router# show ip bgp regexp 300$
```

- Match end of input string, AS_PATH, = 300.
- Originating autonomous system = 300.
- Routes matched: 192.168.2.0.

```
Router# show ip bgp regexp ^200
```

- Match beginning of input string, AS_PATH, = 200.
- Last prepended autonomous system was 200.
- Routes matched: none.

Regular Expressions: Example Two

Use the following output of the **show ip bgp** command to see how different examples of regular expressions can help filter specific patterns.

```
Router#show ip bgp

    Network           Path
*>  192.168.0.0              i
*>  192.168.1.0        100 i
*>  192.168.3.0        100 200
i*> 192.168.4.0         300 i
*>  172.16.0.0         300 400 i
*>  10.0.0.0           300 400 1000 i
```

```
Router#show ip bpg regexp 100
```

- Match input string, AS_PATH, containing 100, including 1000.
- Routes matched: 192.168.1.0, 192.168.3.0, 10.0.0.0.

```
Router#show ip bpg regexp ^100_
```

- Match beginning of input string, AS_PATH, = 100.
- Last prepended autonomous system was 100.
- Routes matched: 192.168.1.0, 192.168.3.0.

BGP Route Filtering Using Access Lists

Figure 6-9 shows the commands necessary to configure route filters using access lists.

Figure 6-9   Network Topology for Route Filter Configuration Using Access Lists

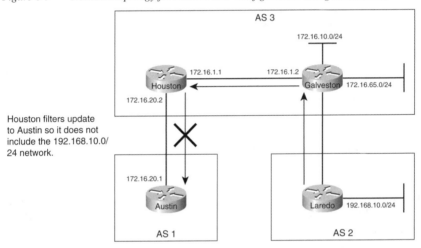

In this scenario, we want to have Houston filter updates to Austin so that it does not include the 192.69.10.0/24 network.

`Houston(config)#`**`router bgp 3`**	Starts the BGP routing process.
`Houston(config-router)#`**`neighbor`** **`172.16.1.2 remote-as 3`**	Identifies a peer router at 172.16.1.2.
`Houston(config-router)#`**`neighbor`** **`172.16.20.1 remote-as 1`**	Identifies a peer router at 172.16.20.1.
`Houston(config-router)#`**`neighbor`** **`172.16.20.1 distribute-list 1 out`**	Applies a filter of ACL 1 to updates sent to neighbor 172.16.20.1.
`Houston(config-router)#`**`exit`**	Returns to global configuration mode.

Houston(config)#**access-list 1 deny 192.168.10.0 0.0.0.255**	Creates the filter to prevent the 192.168.10.0 network from being part of the routing update.
Houston(config)#**access-list 1 permit any**	Creates the filter that allows all other networks to be part of the routing update

TIP: A standard ACL offers limited functionality. If you want to advertise the aggregate address of 172.16.0.0/16 but not the individual subnet, a standard ACL will not work. You need to use an extended ACL.

When you are using extended ACLS with BGP route filters, the extended ACL will first match the network address and *then* match the subnet mask of the prefix. To do this, both the network and the netmask are paired with their own wildcard bitmask:

Router(config)#**access-list 101 permit ip 172.16.0.0 0.0.255.255 255.255.0.0 0.0.0.0**

To help overcome the confusing nature of this syntax, Cisco IOS Software introduced the **ip prefix-list** command in Cisco IOS Release 12.0.

BGP Route Filtering Using Prefix Lists

The general syntax for configuring a prefix list is as follows:

Router(config)#**ip prefix-list** *list-name* [**seq** *seq-value*] **deny**|**permit** *network/len* [**ge** *ge-value*] [**le** *le-value*]

The table that follows describes the parameters for this command.

Parameter	Description
list-name	The name of the prefix list.
seq	(Optional) Applies a sequence number to the entry being created or deleted.
seq-value	(Optional) Specifies the sequence number.
deny	Denies access to matching conditions.
permit	Permits access for matching conditions.
network/len	(Mandatory) The network number and length (in bits) of the netmask.
ge	(Optional) Applies *ge-value* to the range specified.

ge-value	(Optional) Specifies the lesser value of a range (the 'from' portion of the range description).
le	(Optional) Applies *le-value* to the range specified.
le-value	(Optional) Specifies the greater value of a range (the 'to' portion of the range description).

TIP: You must define a prefix list before you can apply it as a route filter.

TIP: There is an **implicit deny** statement at the end of each prefix list.

TIP: The range of sequence numbers that can be entered is from 1 to 4,294,967,294. If a sequence number is not entered when configuring this command, a default sequence numbering is applied to the prefix list. The number 5 is applied to the first prefix entry, and subsequent unnumbered entries are incremented by 5.

A router tests for prefix list matches from the lowest sequence number to the highest.

By numbering your **prefix-list** statements, you can add new entries at any point in the list.

The following examples show how you can use the **prefix-list** command to filter networks from being propagated through BGP.

`Router(config)#ip prefix-list KA-TET permit 172.16.0.0/16`	Creates an IP prefix list for BGP route filtering.
`Router(config)#router bgp 100`	Starts the BGP routing process.
`Router(config-router)#neighbor 192.168.1.1 remote-as 200`	Identifies a peer router at 192.168.1.1.
`Router(config-router)#neighbor 192.168.1.1 prefix-list KA-TET out`	Applies the prefix list named KA-TET to updates sent to this peer.
	This configuration restricts the update to the 172.16.0.0/16 summary. The router will not send a subnet route—such as 172.16.0.0/17 or 172.16.20/24 in an update to autonomous system 200.

`Router(config)#ip prefix-list ROSE permit 192.0.0.0/8 le 24`	Creates a prefix list that will accept a netmask of up to 24 bits (**le** meaning less than or equal to) in routes with the prefix 192.0.0.0/8. Because no sequence number is identified, the default number of 5 is applied.
`Router(config)#ip prefix-list ROSE deny 192.0.0.0/8 ge 25`	Creates a prefix list that will deny routes with a netmask of 25 bits or greater (**ge** meaning greater than or equal to) in routes with the prefix 192.0.0.0/8. Because no sequence number is identified, the number 10 is applied—an increment of 5 over the previous statement.
	This configuration will allow routes such as 192.2.0.0/16 or 192.2.20.0/24 to be permitted, but a more specific subnet such as 192.168.10.128/25 will be denied.
`Router(config)#ip prefix-list TOWER permit 10.0.0.0/8 ge 16 le 24`	Creates a prefix list that permits all prefixes in the 10.0.0.0/8 address space that have a netmask of between 16 and 24 bits (greater than or equal to 16 bits, and less than or equal to 24 bits).
`Router(config)#ip prefix-list SHARDIK seq 5 deny 0.0.0.0/0`	Creates a prefix list and assigns a sequence number of 5 to this statement.
`Router(config)#ip prefix-list SHARDIK seq 10 permit 172.16.0.0/16`	Creates a prefix list and assigns a sequence number of 10 to this statement.
`Router(config)#ip prefix-list SHARDIK seq 15 permit 192.168.0.0/16 le 24`	Creates a prefix list and assigns a sequence number of 15 to this statement.
`Router(config)#no ip prefix-list SHARDIK seq 10`	Removes sequence number 10 from the prefix list.

BGP: Configuration Example

Figure 6-10 shows the network topology for the configuration that follows, which demonstrates a simple BGP network using the commands covered in this chapter.

Figure 6-10   Network Topology for Simple BGP Network

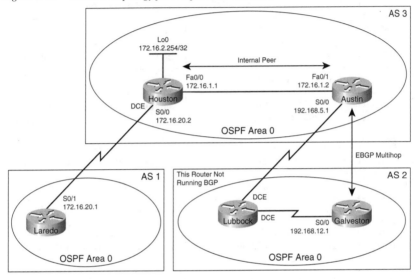

Houston Router

`Router>`**`enable`**	Moves to privileged mode.
`Router#`**`configure terminal`**	Moves to global configuration mode.
`Router(config)#`**`hostname Houston`**	Sets the router name to Houston.
`Houston(config)#`**`interface loopback 0`**	Moves to loopback interface mode.
`Houston(config-if)#`**`ip address 172.16.2.254 255.255.255.255`**	Assigns an IP address and netmask.
`Houston(config-if)#`**`interface fastethernet 0/0`**	Moves to interface configuration mode.
`Houston(config-if)#`**`ip address 172.16.1.1 255.255.255.0`**	Assigns an IP address and netmask.
`Houston(config-if)#`**`no shutdown`**	Activates the interface.

`Houston(config-if)#interface serial 0/0`	Moves to interface configuration mode.
`Houston(config-if)#ip address 172.16.20.2 255.255.255.0`	Assigns an IP address and netmask.
`Houston(config-if)#clock rate 56000`	Assigns the clock rate.
`Houston(config-if)#no shutdown`	Activates the interface.
`Houston(config-if)#exit`	Returns to global configuration mode.
`Houston(config)#router ospf 1`	Starts the OSPF routing process.
`Houston(config-router)#network 172.16.0.0 0.0.255.255 area 0`	Assigns any interface with an address of 172.16.x.x to be placed into OSPF area 0.
`Houston(config-router)#exit`	Returns to global configuration mode.
`Houston(config)#router bgp 3`	Starts the BGP routing process.
`Houston(config-router)#no synchronization`	Turns off route synchronization.
`Houston(config-router)#neighbor 172.16.1.2 remote-as 3`	Identifies a peer router at 172.16.1.2.
`Houston(config-router)#neighbor 172.16.1.2 update-source loopback 0`	Informs the router to use any operational interface for TCP connections, as long as Loopback0 is configured.
`Houston(config-router)#neighbor 172.16.20.1 remote-as 1`	Identifies a peer router at 172.16.20.1.
`Houston(config-router)#no auto-summary`	Disables auto-summarization.
`Houston(config-router)#exit`	Returns to global configuration mode.
`Houston(config)#exit`	Returns to privileged mode.
`Houston#copy running-config startup-config`	Saves the configuration to NVRAM.

Laredo Router

`Router>`**`enable`**	Moves to privileged mode.
`Router#`**`configure terminal`**	Moves to global configuration mode.
`Router(config)#`**`hostname Laredo`**	Sets the router name to Laredo.
`Laredo(config)#`**`interface serial 0/1`**	Moves to interface configuration mode.
`Laredo(config-if)#`**`ip address 172.16.20.1 255.255.255.0`**	Assigns an IP address and netmask.
`Laredo(config-if)#`**`no shutdown`**	Activates the interface.
`Laredo(config-if)#`**`exit`**	Returns to global configuration mode.
`Laredo(config)#`**`router bgp 1`**	Starts the BGP routing process.
`Laredo(config-router)#`**`no synchronization`**	Turns off route synchronization.
`Laredo(config-router)#`**`neighbor 172.16.20.2 remote-as 3`**	Identifies a peer router at 172.16.20.2.
`Laredo(config-router)#`**`no auto-summary`**	Disables auto-summarization.
`Laredo(config-router)#`**`exit`**	Returns to global configuration mode.
`Laredo(config)#`**`exit`**	Returns to privileged mode.
`Laredo#`**`copy running-config startup-config`**	Saves the configuration to NVRAM.

Galveston Router

`Router>`**`enable`**	Moves to privileged mode.
`Router#`**`configure terminal`**	Moves to global configuration mode.
`Router(config)#`**`hostname Galveston`**	Sets router name to Galveston.
`Galveston(config)#`**`interface serial 0/0`**	Moves to interface configuration mode.

Galveston(config-if)#`ip address` `192.168.12.1 255.255.255.0`	Assigns an IP address and netmask.
Galveston(config-if)#`no shutdown`	Activates the interface.
Galveston(config-if)#`exit`	Returns to global configuration mode.
Galveston(config)#`router ospf 1`	Starts the OSPF routing process.
Galveston(config-router)#`network` `192.168.12.0 0.0.0.255 area 0`	Assigns any interface with an address of 192.168.12.x to be placed into OSPF Area 0.
Galveston(config-router)#`exit`	Returns to global configuration mode.
Galveston(config)#`router bgp 2`	Starts the BGP routing process.
Galveston(config-router)#`neighbor` `192.168.5.1 remote-as 3`	Identifies a peer router at 192.168.5.1.
Galveston(config-router)#`neighbor` `192.168.5.1 ebgp-multihop 2`	Allows for two routers that are not directly connected to establish an EBGP session.
Galveston(config-router)#`no auto-summary`	Disables auto summarization.
Galveston(config-router)#`exit`	Returns to global configuration mode.
Galveston(config)#`exit`	Returns to privileged mode.
Galveston#`copy running-config startup-config`	Saves the configuration to NVRAM.

Austin Router

Router>`enable`	Moves to privileged mode.
Router#`configure terminal`	Moves to global configuration mode.
Router(config)#`hostname Austin`	Sets the router name to Austin.
Austin(config)#`interface serial 0/0`	Moves to interface configuration mode.

`Austin(config-if)#`**`ip address 192.168.5.1`** **`255.255.255.0`**	Assigns an IP address and netmask.
`Austin(config-if)#`**`no shutdown`**	Activates the interface.
`Austin(config-if)#`**`interface`** **`fastethernet 0/1`**	Moves to interface configuration mode.
`Austin (config-if)#`**`ip address 172.16.1.2`** **`255.255.255.0`**	Assigns an IP address and netmask.
`Austin(config-if)#`**`no shutdown`**	Activates the interface.
`Austin(config-if)#`**`exit`**	Returns to global configuration mode.
`Austin(config)#`**`router ospf 1`**	Starts the OSPF routing process.
`Austin(config-router)#`**`network`** **`172.16.0.0 0.0.255.255 area 0`**	Assigns any interface with an address of 172.16.$x.x$ to be placed into OSPF area 0.
`Austin(config-router)#`**`network`** **`192.168.5.0 0.0.0.255 area 0`**	Assigns any interface with an address of 192.168.5.x to be placed into OSPF area 0.
`Austin(config-router)#`**`exit`**	Returns to global configuration mode.
`Austin(config)#`**`router bgp 3`**	Starts the BGP routing process.
`Austin(config-router)#`**`no`** **`synchronization`**	Turns off route synchronization.
`Austin(config-router)#`**`neighbor`** **`172.16.2.254 remote-as 3`**	Identifies a peer router at 172.16.2.254.
`Austin(config-router)#`**`neighbor`** **`192.168.12.1 remote-as 2`**	Identifies a peer router at 192.168.12.1.
`Austin(config-router)#`**`neighbor`** **`192.168.12.1 ebgp-multihop 2`**	Allows for two routers that are not directly connected to establish an eBGP session.
`Austin(config-router)#`**`no auto-summary`**	Turns off auto-summarization.
`Austin(config-router)#`**`exit`**	Returns to global configuration mode.
`Austin(config)#`**`exit`**	Returns to privileged mode.
`Austin#`**`copy running-config startup-config`**	Saves the configuration to NVRAM.

CHAPTER 7

Multicast

This chapter provides information and commands concerning the following multicast topics:

- IP multicast address examples
    - Class D addresses
    - Reserved link-local addresses
    - Globally scoped addresses
    - Source specific multicast (SSM) addresses
    - GLOP addresses
    - Limited-scope addresses
    - Layer 2 multicast addresses
    - Ethernet MAC address mapping
- Internet Group Management Protocol (IGMP) snooping
- Verifying multicast addresses
- Cisco Group Management Protocol (CGMP)
- Configuring IP multicast
- Verifying PIM configuration
- Auto-RP
- Defining scope of delivery of multicast packets
- Joining a multicast group
- Changing Internet Group Management Protocol (IGMP) versions
- Verifying IGMP version
- Configuration example: Multicast routing using PIM Sparse-Dense mode

IP Multicast Address Examples

Multicast addresses are unlike unicast addresses in that they do not identify a specific host, but rather a multicast group. Multicast packets are sent to a multicast group address. To receive data sent to a multicast address, a host must therefore join the group that the address identifies. The multicast address range has been subdivided to provide predictable behavior for the different address ranges, and for address reuse within smaller domains.

Class D Addresses

Leading Bit Pattern	1110
Address pattern	1110xxxx.xxxxxxxx.xxxxxxxx.xxxxxxxx
First octet decimal range	224–239
Address range	224.0.0.0 to 239.255.255.255

Reserved Link-Local Addresses

Address range	224.0.0.0 to 224.0.0.255.
Used for	Used by network protocols on a local network segment.

NOTE: A router should never forward packets with these addresses—typically, packets with these addresses have a Time To Live (TTL) of one (1) and are therefore not forwarded.

Some well-known reserved link-local multicast addresses are listed in the following table.

Address	Group
224.0.0.1	All multicast-capable hosts on this segment.
224.0.0.2	All multicast-capable routers on this segment .
224.0.0.4	All Distance Vector Multicast Routing Protocol (DVMRP) routers on this segment.
224.0.0.5	All Open Shortest Path First (OSPF) routers.
224.0.0.6	All OSPF designated routers.
224.0.0.9	All Routing Information Protocol Version 2 (RIPv2) routers.
224.0.0.10	All Enhanced Interior Gateway Routing Protocol (EIGRP) routers.
224.0.0.13	All Protocol Independent Multicast (PIM) routers.
224.0.0.15	All Core Based Tree (CBT) routers.

Globally Scoped Addresses

Address range	224.0.1.0 to 238.255.255.255.
Used to	Multicast data between organizations and across the Internet.

NOTE: Some globally scoped addresses have been registered with Internet Assigned Numbers Authority (IANA)—224.0.1.1 is reserved for Network Time Protocol (NTP).

Source Specific Multicast (SSM) Addresses

Address range	232.0.0.0 to 232.255.255.255.
Used for	SSM is an extension of PIM. SSM allows for the efficient data delivery in one-to-many (broadcast) communications.

NOTE: SSM is a core network technology for the Cisco implementation of IP multicast targeted for audio and video broadcast application environments.

GLOP Addresses

Address range	233.0.0.0 to 233.255.255.255.
Used for	Used statically by organizations that have an autonomous system number registered by a network registry, such as IANA, and listed in the RWhois database. For purposes of GLOP, the IANA has allocated 233/8 as an address space.

NOTE: Consider the autonomous system number 61500. Written in hexadecimal, it would look like F03C. Separating this into two equal parts, you have F0 and 3C. Converting each of these numbers into decimal, you have 240 and 60. Therefore, this autonomous system number would yield a GLOP address of 233.240.60.0/24. Multicast group addresses in this space can be used by the organization with autonomous system 61500 and routed throughout the Internet multicast backbone.

NOTE: GLOP is a word, not an acronym.

Limited-Scope Addresses

Address range	239.0.0.0 to 239.255.255.255.
Used for	Analogous to private IP addresses that are used within the scope of a single organization.

NOTE: Companies use limited-scope addresses to have local multicast applications that will not be forwarded over the Internet. Routers are configured with filters to prevent traffic from leaving the autonomous system.

Layer 2 Multicast Addresses

First 3 bytes	01-00-5E
First 3 bytes in binary	00000001.00000000.01011110
Last 3 bytes	Binary 0 plus last 23 bits copied from the multicast IP address
Last 3 bytes in binary	0xxxxxxx.xxxxxxxx.xxxxxxxx
MAC address in binary	00000001.00000000.01011110.0xxxxxxx.xxxxxxxx.xxxxxxxx

Ethernet MAC Address Mapping

This Address	Equates To
Multicast address 224.10.8.5	MAC address 01-00-5E-0A-08-05
224.10.8.5	11100000000010100000100000000101
.	11100000*00010100000100000000101*
.	**0** is the fixed binary 0, and *00010100000100000000101* is the last 23 bits of the multicast IP address
MAC address 00000001.00000000.010111 10.00001010.00001000.000 00101	01-00-5E-0A-08-05

CAUTION: In a 32-bit multicast address, the first 4 bits are fixed at 1110. Because all multicast addresses are fixed to this pattern, this part of the address does not need to be in the MAC address. The last 23 bits are translated into the MAC address. That leaves 5 bits that are not translated. These 5 bits are represented by question marks (?) in the following example.

Layer 3 address: 12345678.12345678.12345678.12345678

Bit value: 1110????.?*xxxxxxx.xxxxxxxx.xxxxxxxx*

where x = bits translated into MAC

CAUTION: This method for mapping Layer 3 multicast addresses to Layer 2 MAC addresses results in 32 (2^5) Layer 3 addresses that can be mapped to each multicast MAC address. For example, all of the following can be mapped to 0x01-00-5E-01-01-02:

224.1.1.2

224.129.1.2

225.1.1.2

225.129.1.2

226.1.1.2

226.129.1.2

...

238.1.1.2

238.129.1.2

239.1.1.2

239.129.1.2

MAC: 01-00-5E-01-01-02 =
00000001.00000000.01011110.0*0000001.00000001.00000010*

IP:

1110 **0000.0** 0000001.00000001.00000010

1110 **0000.1** 0000001.00000001.00000010

1110 **0001.0** 0000001.00000001.00000010

...

1110 **1111.1** 0000001.00000001.00000010

Therefore, it is recommended to *avoid* overlapping when implementing multicast applications by tuning the destination IP address at the application layer.

CAUTION: Remember that switches forward frames based on MAC addresses. If a switch is configured for Layer 2 multicast snooping, it will forward frames to all members corresponding to the other IP multicast addresses of the same MAC address mapping, even if the frames belong to a different IP multicast group. Most Layer 2 switches flood all multicast traffic that falls within the MAC address range of 0x0100.5E00.00*xx* to all ports on the switch even if IGMP snooping is enabled.

Internet Group Management Protocol (IGMP) Snooping

`Switch(config)#ip igmp snooping`	Globally enables IGMP snooping on all existing VLAN interfaces.
	NOTE: By default, IGMP snooping is globally enabled on the switch.
`Switch(config)#no ip igmp snooping`	Globally disables IGMP snooping, to allow for IGMP snooping on specific VLAN interfaces.
	TIP: When IGMP snooping is globally enabled, it enables IGMP snooping on all the existing VLAN interfaces. When IGMP snooping is globally disabled, it disables IGMP snooping on all the existing VLAN interfaces. IGMP snooping can then be enabled on a per-VLAN basis with the **ip igmp snooping vlan** x command.
`Switch(config)#ip igmp snooping vlan x`	Enables IGMP snooping for a specific VLAN on VLAN x. The range of VLAN IDs is 1 to 1001.
	TIP: Global IGMP snooping overrides VLAN IGMP snooping.
`Router(config)#ip igmp snooping vlan x mrouter learn pim-dvmrp`	The router will listen to PIM-DVMRP packets to determine multicast router ports.
	NOTE: PIM-DVMRP is the default multicast router learning method.
`Router(config)#ip igmp snooping vlan x mrouter interface interface-id`	Specifies the multicast router VLAN ID and specifies the interface to the multicast router.
	NOTE: The interface is a physical interface. Port channels were allowed up through Cisco IOS Software Release 12.2. The port channel range is 1 to 12.
`Switch(config)#ip igmp snooping vlan x static mac-address interface interface-id`	Statically configures a Layer 2 port as a member of a multicast group. x is the multicast group VLAN ID. *mac-address* is the static group MAC address. *interface-id* is the interface configured to a static router port.

Switch(config)#`ip igmp snooping vlan x immediate-leave`	Enables the IGMP immediate leave process on VLAN x.
	NOTE: Immediate leave is supported with only IGMP Version 2 hosts.

Verifying Multicast Addressing

Switch#`show mac-address-table multicast`	Displays the entire MAC address table.
Switch#`show mac-address-table multicast vlan x`	Displays the MAC address table for VLAN x.

Cisco Group Management Protocol (CGMP)

Router(config)#`interface fastethernet 0/0`	Enters interface configuration mode.
Router(config-if)#`ip cgmp`	Enables CGMP. This command should be used only on 802 media (Ethernet, FDDI, Token Ring) or ATM.

Configuring IP Multicast

Router(config)#`ip multicast-routing`	Enables IP multicast routing.
Router(config)#`interface fastethernet 0/0`	Enters interface config mode.
Router(config-if)#`ip pim dense-mode`	Enables PIM dense mode on the interface.
Router(config-if)#`ip pim sparse-mode`	Enables PIM sparse mode on the interface.
Router(config-if)#`ip pim sparse-dense-mode`	Enables PIM to operate in sparse or dense mode, depending on the group.

`Router(config-if)#exit`	Returns to global configuration mode.
`Router(config)#ip pim rp-address w.x.y.z`	Configures the address of a PIM rendezvous point (RP).

Verifying PIM Configuration

`Router#show ip pim interface`	Displays information about all interfaces configured for PIM.
`Router#show ip pim interface fastethernet 0/0`	Displays information for specific interface.
`Router#show ip pim interface count`	Displays the number of packets sent and received out all interfaces.
`Router#show ip pim neighbor`	Displays all discovered PIM neighbors.
`Router#show ip pim neighbor fastethernet 0/0`	Displays all PIM neighbors discovered out interface fastethernet 0/0.

Auto-RP

`Router(config)#ip pim send-rp-announce type number scope ttl group-list acl#`	Enables auto-RP on this router. *type number* refers to the interface type and number that identifies the RP address. **scope** *ttl* is the Time-To-Live value that limits the announcements. **group-list** *acl#* points to a standard ACL that describes the group ranges for which this router is the RP.

`Router(config)#ip pim send-rp-announce fastethernet 0/0 scope 28 group list 15` `Router(config)#access-list 15 permit 224.0.0.0 15.255.255.255`	RP announcements will be sent out all PIM-enabled interfaces for a maximum of 28 hops. The IP address of fastethernet 0/0 will be the address by which the RP is identified. Access control list (ACL) 15 describes which groups this router serves as RP.
`Router(config)#ip pim send-rp-discovery` *`type number`* `scope` *`ttl`*	Configures the router to be an RP-mapping agent. *type number* is the interface type and number that identifies the RP mapping agent address (optional). **scope** *ttl* is a value that keeps discovery messages within this number of hops.
`Router(config)#ip pim send-rp-discovery scope 18`	Sends Auto-RP Discovery messages out all PIM interfaces but limits the message to 18 hops.

Defining Scope of Delivery of Multicast Packets

`Router(config)#interface fastethernet 0/0`	Moves to interface configuration mode.
`Router(config-if)#ip multicast ttl-threshold` *`x`*	Specifies a Time-To-Live value from 0 to 255, expressed in hops.
	NOTE: The default value is 0, meaning that all multicast packets are forwarded out the interface. The higher the number, the higher the threshold value. For example, a threshold set to 175 means that multicast packets must have a TTL greater than 175 to be forwarded out this interface.

	TIP: You should configure the TTL threshold only on border routers.
	TIP: This command replaces the **ip multicast-threshold** command, which is now obsolete.

Joining a Multicast Group

`Router(config)#interface fastethernet 0/0`	Moves to interface configuration mode.
`Router(config-if)#ip igmp join-group 227.1.1.1`	Allows the router to join the multicast group identified by the group address of 227.1.1.1.

Changing Internet Group Management Protocol (IGMP) Versions

`Router(config)#interface fastethernet 0/0`	Moves to interface configuration mode.
`Router(config-if)#ip igmp version 3`	Selects IGMP Version 3.
	NOTE: One advantage of IGMPv3 is that it allows hosts to indicate that they want to receive traffic only from particular sources within a multicast group. IGMPv3 adds the ability to filter multicasts based on the multicast source.
`Router(config-if)#ip igmp version 2`	Selects IGMP Version 2.
`Router(config-if)#ip igmp version 1`	Selects IGMP Version 1.
	NOTE: The default version is Version 2.

Verifying IGMP Version

`Router#show ip igmp interface fastethernet 0/0`	Shows the current version setting for the specified interface.

Configuration Example: Multicast Routing Using PIM Sparse-Dense Mode

Figure 7-1 shows the network topology for the configuration that follows, which demonstrates how to configure multicast routing with PIM-Sparse-Dense mode using the commands covered in this chapter.

Figure 7-1   *Network Topology for Configuring Multicast Routing Using PIM Sparse-Dense Mode*

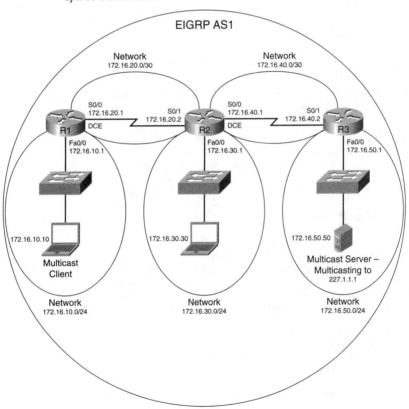

R1 Router

`Router>`**`enable`**	Moves to privileged mode.
`Router#`**`configure terminal`**	Moves to global configuration mode.
`Router(config)#`**`hostname R1`**	Assigns a host name to the router.
`R1(config)#`**`ip multicast-routing`**	Enables IP multicast routing.
`R1(config)#`**`interface fastethernet 0/0`**	Enters interface configuration mode.
`R1(config-if)#`**`ip address 172.16.10.1 255.255.255.0`**	Assigns an IP address and netmask.
`R1(config-if)#`**`ip pim sparse-dense-mode`**	Enables PIM Sparse-Dense mode.
`R1(config-if)#`**`ip igmp join-group 227.1.1.1`**	Allows the router to join the multicast group identified by the group address of 227.1.1.1.
`R1(config-if)#`**`no shutdown`**	Starts the interface.
`R1(config-if)#`**`interface serial 0/0`**	Moves to interface configuration mode.
`R1(config-if)#`**`ip address 172.16.20.1 255.255.255.252`**	Assigns an IP address and netmask.
`R1(config-if)#`**`ip pim sparse-dense-mode`**	Enables PIM Sparse-Dense mode.
`R1(config-if)#`**`clock rate 56000`**	Sets the clock rate.
`R1(config-if)#`**`no shutdown`**	Starts the interface.
`R1(config-if)#`**`exit`**	Returns to global configuration mode.
`R1(config)#`**`router eigrp 1`**	Enables the EIGRP routing process.
`R1(config-router)#`**`network 172.16.0.0`**	Advertises directly connected networks (classful address only).
`R1(config-router)#`**`no auto-summary`**	Disables auto-summarization.
`R1(config-router)#`**`exit`**	Returns to global configuration mode.
`R1(config)#`**`exit`**	Returns to privileged mode.
`R1#`**`copy running-config startup-config`**	Saves the configuration to NVRAM.

R2 Router

`Router>`**`enable`**	Moves to privileged mode.
`Router#`**`configure terminal`**	Moves to global configuration mode.
`Router(config)#`**`hostname R2`**	Assigns a host name to the router.
`R2(config)#`**`ip multicast-routing`**	Enables IP multicast routing.
`R2(config)#`**`interface fastethernet 0/0`**	Enters interface configuration mode.
`R2(config-if)#`**`ip address 172.16.30.1 255.255.255.0`**	Assigns an IP address and netmask.
`R2(config-if)#`**`ip pim sparse-dense-mode`**	Enables PIM Sparse-Dense mode.
`R2(config-if)#`**`no shutdown`**	Starts the interface.
`R2(config-if)#`**`interface serial 0/1`**	Moves to interface configuration mode.
`R2(config-if)#`**`ip address 172.16.20.2 255.255.255.252`**	Assigns an IP address and netmask.
`R2(config-if)#`**`ip pim sparse-dense-mode`**	Enables PIM Sparse-Dense mode.
`R2(config-if)#`**`no shutdown`**	Starts the interface.
`R2(config-if)#`**`interface serial 0/0`**	Moves to interface configuration mode.
`R2(config-if)#`**`ip address 172.16.40.1 255.255.255.252`**	Assigns an IP address and netmask.
`R2(config-if)#`**`ip pim sparse-dense-mode`**	Enables PIM Sparse-Dense mode.
`R2(config-if)#`**`clock rate 56000`**	Sets the clock rate.
`R2(config-if)#`**`no shutdown`**	Starts the interface.
`R2(config-if)#`**`exit`**	Returns to global configuration mode.
`R2(config)#`**`router eigrp 1`**	Enables the EIGRP routing process.
`R2(config-router)#`**`network 172.16.0.0`**	Advertises directly connected networks (classful address only).
`R2(config-router)#`**`no auto-summary`**	Disables auto-summarization.

`R2(config-router)#exit`	Returns to global configuration mode.
`R2(config)#exit`	Returns to privileged mode.
`R2#copy running-config startup-config`	Saves the configuration to NVRAM.

R3 Router

`Router>enable`	Moves to privileged mode.
`Router#configure terminal`	Moves to global configuration mode.
`Router(config)#hostname R3`	Assigns a host name to the router.
`R3(config)#ip multicast-routing`	Enables IP multicast routing.
`R3(config)#interface serial 0/1`	Enters interface configuration mode.
`R3(config-if)#ip address 172.16.40.2 255.255.255.252`	Assigns an IP address and netmask.
`R3(config-if)#ip pim sparse-dense-mode`	Enables PIM Sparse-Dense mode.
`R3(config-if)#no shutdown`	Starts the interface.
`R3(config-if)#interface fastethernet 0/0`	Moves to interface configuration mode.
`R3(config-if)#ip address 172.16.50.1 255.255.255.0`	Assigns an IP address and netmask.
`R3(config-if)#ip pim sparse-dense-mode`	Enables PIM Sparse-Dense mode.
`R3(config-if)#no shutdown`	Starts the interface.
`R3(config-if)#exit`	Returns to global configuration mode.
`R3(config)#router eigrp 1`	Enables the EIGRP routing process.
`R3(config-router)#network 172.16.0.0`	Advertises directly connected networks (classful address only).
`R3(config-router)#no auto-summary`	Disables auto-summarization.
`R3(config-router)#exit`	Returns to global configuration mode.
`R3(config)#exit`	Returns to privileged mode.
`R3#copy running-config startup-config`	Saves the configuration to NVRAM.

CHAPTER 8

IPv6

This chapter provides information and commands concerning the following IPv6 topics:

- Assigning IPv6 addresses to interfaces
- Cisco Express Forwarding (CEF) and distributed CEF switching for IPv6
- IPv6 and OSPFv3
  - Enabling OSPF for IPv6 on an interface
  - OSPFv3 and stub/NSSA areas
  - Enabling an OSPF for IPv6 area range
  - Enabling an IPv4 router ID for OSPFv3
  - Forcing an SPF calculation
- Configuration example: OSPFv3
- IPv6 tunnels: Manual overlay
- Static routes in IPv6
- Floating static routes in IPv6
- Verifying and troubleshooting IPv6
- IPv6 ping utility

> **NOTE:** For an excellent overview of IPv6, I strongly recommend you read Jeff Doyle's book, *Routing TCP/IP,* Volume I, Second Edition.

Assigning IPv6 Addresses to Interfaces

Router(config)#**ipv6 unicast-routing**	Enables the forwarding of IPv6 unicast datagrams globally on the router.
Router(config)#**interface fast Ethernet 0/0**	Moves to interface configuration mode.
Router(config-if)#**ipv6 enable**	Automatically configures an IPv6 link-local address on the interface and enables IPv6 processing on the interface.
	NOTE: The link-local address that the **ipv6 enable** command configures can be used only to communicate with nodes on the same link.

`Router(config-if)#ipv6 address 3000::1/64`	Configures a global IPv6 address on the interface and enables IPv6 processing on the interface.
`Router(config-if)#ipv6 address 2001:db8:0:1::/64 eui-64`	Configures a global IPv6 address with an interface identifier in the low-order 64 bits of the IPv6 address.
`Router(config-if)#ipv6 address fe80::260:3eff:fe47:1530/64 link-local`	Configures a specific link-local IPv6 address on the interface rather than the one that is automatically configured when IPv6 is enabled on the interface.
`Router(config-if)#ipv6 unnumbered type/number`	Specifies an unnumbered interface and enables IPv6 processing on the interface. The global IPv6 address of the interface specified by *type/number* will be used as the source address.

Cisco Express Forwarding (CEF) and Distributed CEF Switching for IPv6

`Router(config)#ipv6 cef`	Enables CEFv6 globally on the router.
	NOTE: You must enable CEFv4 globally on the router by using the **ip cef** global configuration command before enabling CEFv6 globally on the router.
	NOTE: The **ipv6 cef** command is not supported on the Cisco 12000 series Internet routers because this distributed platform operates only in dCEFv6 mode.
`Router(config)#ipv6 cef distributed`	Enables dCEFv6 globally on the router.
	NOTE: You must enable dCEFv4 by using the **ip cef distributed** global configuration command before enabling dCEFv6 globally on the router.

	NOTE: The **ipv6 cef distributed** command is not supported on the Cisco 12000 series Internet routers because dCEFv6 is enabled by default on this platform.
`Router(config)#ipv6 cef accounting per-prefix`	Enables CEFv6 and dCEFv6 network accounting globally on the router. The keyword **per-prefix** enables the collection of the number of packets and bytes express forwarded to an IPv6 destination or IPv6 prefix.
`Router(config)#ipv6 cef accounting prefix-length`	Enables CEFv6 and dCEFv6 network accounting globally on the router. The keyword **prefix-length** enables the collection of the number of packets and bytes forwarded to an IPv6 prefix length.
	NOTE: When CEFv6 is enabled globally on the router, accounting information is collected at the route processor (RP); when dCEFv6 is enabled globally on the router, accounting information is collected at the line cards.

IPv6 and OSPFv3

Working with IPv6 requires modifications to any dynamic protocol. The current version of Open Shortest Path First (OSPF), OSPFv2, was developed back in the late 1980s, when some parts of OSPF were designed to compensate for the inefficiencies of routers at that time. Now that router technology has dramatically increased, rather than modify OSPFv2 for IPv6, it was decided to create a new version of OSPF—OSPFv3—not just for IPv6, but for other, newer technologies, too. This section covers using IPv6 with OSPFv3.

Enabling OSPF for IPv6 on an Interface

`Router(config)#interface fastethernet 0/0`	Moves to interface configuration mode.
`Router(config-if)# ipv6 address 2001:db8:0:1::/64`	Configures a global IPv6 address on the interface and enables IPv6 processing on the interface.
`Router(config-if)#ipv6 ospf 1 area 0`	Enables OSPFv3 process 1 on the interface and places this interface into area 0.
	NOTE: The OSPFv3 process is created automatically when OSPFv3 is enabled on an interface.
	NOTE: The **ipv6 ospf** *x* **area** *y* command has to be configured on each interface that will take part in OSPFv3.
`Router(config-if)#ipv6 ospf priority 30`	Assigns a priority number to this interface for use in the designated router (DR) election. The priority can be a number from 0 to 255. The default is 1. A router with a priority set to 0 is ineligible to become the DR or the backup DR (BDR).
`Router(config-if)#ipv6 ospf cost 20`	Assigns a cost value of 20 to this interface. The cost value can be an integer value from 1 to 65,535.

OSPFv3 and Stub/NSSA Areas

`Router(config)#ipv6 router ospf`	Creates the OSPFv3 process if it has not already been created, and moves to router configuration mode.
`Router(config-router)#area 1 stub`	The router is configured to be part of a stub area.
`Router(config-router)#area 1 stub no-summary`	The router is configured to be in a totally stubby area. This router is the Area Border Router (ABR) due to the **no-summary** keyword.
`Router(config-router)#area 1 nssa`	The router is configured to be in a not-so-stubby area (NSSA).

`Router(config-router)#`**`area 1 nssa no`** **`summary`**	The router is configured to be in a totally stubby, NSSA area. This router is the ABR due to the **no-summary** keyword.

Enabling an OSPF for IPv6 Area Range

`Router(config)#`**`ipv6 router ospf`**	Creates the OSPFv3 process if it has not already been created, and moves to router configuration mode
`Router(config-router)#`**`area 1 range`** **`2001:db8::/48`**	Consolidates and summarizes routes at an area boundary

Enabling an IPv4 Router ID for OSPFv3

`Router(config)#`**`ipv6 router ospf`**	Creates the OSPFv3 process if it has not already been created, and moves to router configuration mode.
`Router(config-router)#`**`router-id`** **`192.168.254.255`**	Creates an IPv4 32-bit router ID for this router.
	NOTE: In OSPF for IPv6, it is possible that no IPv4 addresses will be configured on any interface. In this case, the user must use the **router-id** command to configure a router ID before the OSPF process will be started. If an IPv4 address does exist when OSPF for IPv6 is enabled on an interface, that IPv4 address is used for the router ID. If more than one IPv4 address is available, a router ID is chosen using the same rules as for OSPF Version 2.

Forcing an SPF Calculation

Router#**clear ipv6 ospf 1 process**	The OSPF database is cleared and repopulated, and then the SPF algorithm is performed.
Router#**clear ipv6 ospf 1 force-spf**	The OSPF database is not cleared; just an SPF calculation is performed.

CAUTION: As with OSPFv2, clearing the OSPFv3 database and forcing a recalculation of the Shortest Path First (SPF) algorithm is processor intensive and should be used with caution.

Configuration Example: OSPFv3

Figure 8-1 shows the network topology for the configuration that follows, which demonstrates how to configure IPv6 and OSPFv3 using the commands covered in this chapter.

Figure 8-1   Network Topology for IPv6 and OSPFv3 Configuration

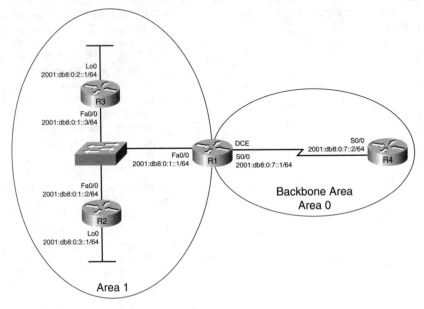

R3 Router

`Router>`**`enable`**	Moves to privileged mode.
`Router#`**`configure terminal`**	Moves to global configuration mode.
`Router(config)#`**`hostname R3`**	Assigns a host name to the router.
`R3(config)#`**`ipv6 unicast-routing`**	Enables the forwarding of IPv6 unicast datagrams globally on the router.
`R3(config)#`**`interface fastethernet 0/0`**	Moves to interface configuration mode.
`R3(config-if)#`**`ipv6 address 2001:db8:0:1::3/64`**	Configures a global IPv6 address on the interface and enables IPv6 processing on the interface.
`R3(config-if)#`**`ipv6 ospf 1 area 1`**	Enables OSPFv3 on the interface and places this interface into area 1.
`R3(config-if)#`**`no shutdown`**	Activates the interface.
`R3(config-if)#`**`interface loopback 0`**	Moves to interface configuration mode.
`R3(config-if)#`**`ipv6 address 2001:db8:0:2::1/64`**	Configures a global IPv6 address on the interface and enables IPv6 processing on the interface.
`R3(config-if)#`**`ipv6 ospf 1 area 1`**	Enables OSPFv3 on the interface and places this interface into area 1.
`R3(config-if)#`**`exit`**	Moves to global configuration mode.
`R3(config)#`**`exit`**	Moves to privileged mode.
`R3#`**`copy running-config startup-config`**	Saves the configuration to NVRAM.

R2 Router

`Router>`**`enable`**	Moves to privileged mode.
`Router#`**`configure terminal`**	Moves to global configuration mode.
`Router(config)#`**`hostname R2`**	Assigns a host name to the router.

`R2(config)#ipv6 unicast-routing`	Enables the forwarding of IPv6 unicast datagrams globally on the router.
`R2(config)#interface fasthethernet 0/0`	Moves to interface configuration mode.
`R2(config-if)#ipv6 address 2001:db8:0:1::2/64`	Configures a global IPv6 addresses on the interface and enables IPv6 processing on the interface.
`R2(config-if)#ipv6 ospf 1 area 1`	Enables OSPFv3 on the interface and places this interface into area 1.
`R2(config-if)#no shutdown`	Starts the interface.
`R2(config-if)#interface loopback 0`	Moves to interface configuration mode.
`R2(config-if)#ipv6 address 2001:db8:0:3::1/64`	Configures a global IPv6 address on the interface and enables IPv6 processing on the interface.
`R2(config-if)#ipv6 ospf 1 area 1`	Enables OSPFv3 on the interface and places this interface into area 1.
`R2(config-if)#no shutdown`	Starts the interface.
`R2(config-if)#exit`	Moves to global configuration mode.
`R2(config)#exit`	Moves to privileged mode.
`R2#copy running-config startup-config`	Saves the configuration to NVRAM.

R1 Router

`Router>enable`	Moves to privileged mode.
`Router#configure terminal`	Moves to global configuration mode.
`Router(config)#hostname R1`	Assigns a host name to the router.
`R1(config)#ipv6 unicast-routing`	Enables the forwarding of IPv6 unicast datagrams globally on the router.
`R1(config)#interface fastethernet 0/0`	Moves to interface configuration mode.

`R1(config-if)#ipv6 address 2001:db8:0:1::1/64`	Configures a global IPv6 address on the interface and enables IPv6 processing on the interface.
`R1(config-if)#ipv6 ospf 1 area 1`	Enables OSPFv3 on the interface and places this interface into area 1.
`R1(config-if)#no shutdown`	Starts the interface.
`R1(config-if)#interface serial 0/0`	Moves to interface configuration mode.
`R1(config-if)#ipv6 address 2001:db8:0:7::1/64`	Configures a global IPv6 address on the interface and enables IPv6 processing on the interface.
`R1(config-if)#ipv6 ospf 1 area 0`	Enables OSPFv3 on the interface and places this interface into area 0.
`R1(config-if)#clock rate 56000`	Assigns a clock rate to this interface.
`R1(config-if)#no shutdown`	Starts the interface.
`R1(config-if)#exit`	Moves to global configuration mode.
`R1(config)#exit`	Moves to privileged mode.
`R1#copy running-config startup-config`	Saves the configuration to NVRAM.

R4 Router

`Router>enable`	Moves to privileged mode.
`Router#configure terminal`	Moves to global configuration mode.
`Router(config)#hostname R4`	Assigns a host name to the router.
`R4(config)#ipv6 unicast-routing`	Enables the forwarding of IPv6 unicast datagrams globally on the router.
`R4(config)#interface serial 0/0`	Moves to interface configuration mode.
`R4(config-if)#ipv6 address 2001:db8:0:7::2/64`	Configures a global IPv6 address on the interface and enables IPv6 processing on the interface.
`R4(config-if)#ipv6 ospf 1 area 0`	Enables OSPFv3 on the interface and places this interface into area 1.

R4(config-if)#**no shutdown**	Starts the interface.
R4(config-if)#**exit**	Moves to global configuration mode.
R4(config)#**exit**	Moves to privileged mode.
R4#**copy running-config startup-config**	Saves the configuration to NVRAM.

IPv6 Tunnels: Manual Overlay

Figure 8-2 shows the network topology for the configuration that follows, which demonstrates how IPv6 tunnels are created.

Figure 8-2   Network Topology for IPv6 Tunnel Configuration

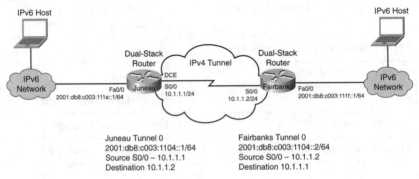

Juneau Router

Router>**enable**	Moves to privileged mode.
Router#**configure terminal**	Moves to global configuration mode.
Router(config)#**hostname Juneau**	Sets the host name of the router.
Juneau(config)#**ipv6 unicast-routing**	Enables the forwarding of IPv6 unicast datagrams globally on the router.
Juneau(config)#**ip cef**	Enables CEFv4 globally on the router.
Juneau(config)#**ipv6 cef**	Enables CEFv6 globally on the router.
Juneau(config)#**interface tunnel0**	Moves to tunnel interface configuration mode.

`Juneau(config-if)#`**`ipv6 address`** **`2001:db8:c003:1104::1/64`**	Assigns the IPv6 address to this interface.
`Juneau(config-if)#`**`tunnel source serial`** **`0/0`**	Specifies the source interface type and number for the tunnel interface.
`Juneau(config-if)#`**`tunnel destination`** **`10.1.1.2`**	Specifies the destination IPv4 address for the tunnel interface.
`Juneau(config-if)#`**`tunnel mode ipv6ip`**	Specifies a manual IPv6 tunnel—specifically that IPv6 is the passenger protocol and IPv4 is both the encapsulation and protocol for the IPv6 tunnel.
`Juneau(config-if)#`**`interface`** **`fastethernet 0/0`**	Moves to interface configuration mode.
`Juneau(config-if)#`**`ipv6 address`** **`2001:db8:c003:111e::1/64`**	Assigns an IPv6 address to this interface.
`Juneau(config-if)#`**`no shutdown`**	Starts the interface.
`Juneau(config-if)#`**`interface serial 0/0`**	Moves to interface configuration mode.
`Juneau(config-if)#`**`ip address 10.1.1.1`** **`255.255.255.252`**	Assigns an IPv4 address and netmask.
`Juneau(config-if)#`**`clock rate 56000`**	Sets the clock rate on the interface.
`Juneau(config-if)#`**`no shutdown`**	Starts the interface.
`Juneau(config-if)#`**`exit`**	Moves to global configuration mode.
`Juneau(config)#`**`exit`**	Moves to privileged mode.
`Juneau#`**`copy running-config startup-config`**	Saves the configuration to NVRAM.

Fairbanks Router

`Router>`**`enable`**	Moves to privileged mode.
`Router#`**`configure terminal`**	Moves to global configuration mode.
`Router(config)#`**`hostname Fairbanks`**	Sets the host name of the router.

`Fairbanks(config)#ipv6 unicast-routing`	Enables the forwarding of IPv6 unicast datagrams globally on the router.
`Fairbanks(config)#ip cef`	Enables CEFv4 globally on the router.
`Fairbanks(config)#ipv6 cef`	Enables CEFv6 globally on the router.
`Fairbanks(config)#interface tunnel0`	Moves to tunnel interface configuration mode.
`Fairbanks(config-if)#ipv6 address 2001:db8:c003:1104::2/64`	Assigns an IPv6 address to this interface.
`Fairbanks(config-if)#tunnel source serial 0/0`	Specifies the source interface type and number for the tunnel interface.
`Fairbanks(config-if)#tunnel destination 10.1.1.1`	Specifies the destination IPv4 address for the tunnel interface.
`Fairbanks(config-if)#tunnel mode ipv6ip`	Specifies a manual IPv6 tunnel—specifically that IPv6 is the passenger protocol and IPv4 is both the encapsulation and protocol for the IPv6 tunnel.
`Fairbanks(config-if)#interface fastethernet 0/0`	Moves to interface configuration mode.
`Fairbanks(config-if)#ipv6 address 2001:db8:c003:111f::1/64`	Assigns an IPv6 address to this interface.
`Fairbanks(config-if)#no shut`	Starts the interface.
`Fairbanks(config-if)#interface serial 0/0`	Moves to serial interface configuration mode.
`Fairbanks(config-if)#ip address 10.1.1.2 255.255.255.252`	Assigns an IPv4 address and netmask.
`Fairbanks(config-if)#no shutdown`	Starts the interface.
`Fairbanks(config-if)#exit`	Moves to global configuration mode.
`Fairbanks(config)#exit`	Moves to privileged mode.
`Fairbanks#copy running-config startup-config`	Saves the configuration to NVRAM.

Static Routes in IPv6

Figure 8-3 shows the network topology for the configuration that follows, which demonstrates how to configure static routes with IPv6.

Figure 8-3   Network Topology for IPv6 Static Routes

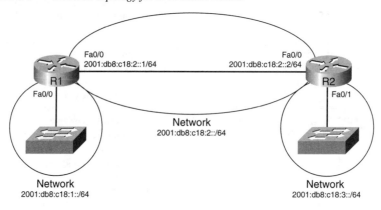

`R1(config)#ipv6 route 2001:db8:c18:3::/64` `2001:db8:c18:2::2/64`	Creates a static route configured to send all packets to a next hop address of 2001:db8:c18:2::2.
`R1(config)#ipv6 route 2001:db8:c18:3::/64` `fastethernet 0/0`	Creates a directly attached static route configured to send packets out interface fastethernet 0/0.
`R1(config)#ipv6 route 2001:db8:c18:3::/64` `fastethernet 0/0 2001:db8:c18:2::2`	Creates a fully specified static route on a broadcast interface.

Floating Static Routes in IPv6

`R1(config)# ipv6 route 2001:db8:c18:3::/64` `fastethernet 0/0 200`	Creates a static route with an administrative distance (AD) set to 200, as opposed to a default AD of 1.
	NOTE: The default ADs used in IPv4 are the same for IPv6.

Verifying and Troubleshooting IPv6

`Router#clear ipv6 route *`	Deletes all routes from the IPv6 routing table.
	NOTE: Clearing all routes from the routing table will cause high CPU utilization rates as the routing table is rebuilt.
`Router#clear ipv6 route 2001:db8:c18:3::/64`	Clears this specific route from the IPv6 routing table.
`Router#clear ipv6 traffic`	Resets IPv6 traffic counters.
`Router#debug ipv6 cef {drop | events | hash | receive | table}`	Displays debug messages for all CEFv6 and dCEFv6 packets as specified by the keywords **drop**, **events**, **hash**, **receive**, or **table**.
	CAUTION: Using the **debug** command can severely affect router performance and can even cause the router to reboot. Caution should always be taken when using the **debug** command. Do not leave **debug** on. Use it long enough to gather needed information, and then disable debugging with the **undebug all** command.
`Router#debug ipv6 ospf adjacencies`	Displays debug messages about the OSPF adjacency process.
`Router#debug ipv6 packet`	Displays debug messages for IPv6 packets.
	TIP: Send your **debug** output to a syslog server to ensure that you have a copy of it in case your router is overloaded and needs to reboot.
`Router#debug ipv6 routing`	Displays debug messages for IPv6 routing table updates and route cache updates.
`Router#show ipv6 cef`	Displays entries in the IPv6 Forwarding Information Base (FIB).
`Router#show ipv6 cef summary`	Displays a summary of the entries in the IPv6 FIB.

Router#**show ipv6 interface**	Displays the status of interfaces configured for IPv6.
Router#**show ipv6 interface brief**	Displays a summarized status of interfaces configured for IPv6.
Router#**show ipv6 neighbors**	Displays IPv6 neighbor discovery cache information.
Router#**show ipv6 ospf**	Displays general information about the OSPFv3 routing process.
Router#**show ipv6 ospf border-routers**	Displays the internal OSPF routing table entries to an ABR or Autonomous System Boundary Router (ASBR).
Router#**show ipv6 ospf database**	Displays OSPFv3-related database information.
Router#**show ipv6 ospf database database-summary**	Displays how many of each type of link-state advertisements (LSA) exist for each area in the database.
Router#**show ipv6 ospf interface**	Displays OSPFv3-related interface information.
Router#**show ipv6 ospf neighbor**	Displays OSPFv3-related neighbor information.
Router#**show ipv6 ospf virtual-links**	Displays parameters and the current state of OSPFv3 virtual links.
Router#**show ipv6 protocols**	Displays the parameters and current state of the active IPv6 routing protocol processes.
Router#**show ipv6 route**	Displays the current IPv6 routing table.
Router#**show ipv6 route summary**	Displays a summarized form of the current IPv6 routing table.
Router#**show ipv6 routers**	Displays IPv6 router advertisement information received from other routers.
Router#**show ipv6 static**	Displays only static IPv6 routes installed in the routing table.
Router#**show ipv6 static 2001:db8:5555:0/16**	Displays only static route information about the specific address given.

Router#show ipv6 static interface s0/0	Displays only static route information with the specified interface as the outgoing interface.
Router#show ipv6 static detail	Displays a more detailed entry for IPv6 static routes.
Router#show ipv6 traffic	Displays statistics about IPv6 traffic.
Router#show ipv6 tunnel	Displays IPv6 tunnel information.

IPv6 Ping

| Router#ping ipv6 2001:db8::3/64 | Diagnoses basic network connectivity using IPv6 to the specified address. |

NOTE: The following table lists the characters that can be displayed as output when using ping in IPv6.

Character	Description
!	Receipt of a reply.
.	Network server timed out while waiting for a reply.
?	Unknown error.
@	Unreachable for unknown reason.
A	Administratively unreachable. This usually means that an access control list (ACL) is blocking traffic.
B	Packet too big.
H	Host unreachable.
N	Network unreachable (beyond scope).
P	Port unreachable.
R	Parameter problem.
T	Time exceeded.
U	No route to host.

Create Your Own Journal Here

Even though I have tried to be as complete as possible in this reference guide, invariably I will have left something out that you need in your specific day-to-day activities. That is why this section is here. Use these blank lines to enter in your own notes, making this reference guide your own personalized journal.